SPLIT QUOTATION

STRANGE HOUSES

Selected Poems by

GONZALO MILLAN

Translated by Annegret Nill

ISBN 1-895006-06-6

Cover design: Bayne Herrera Graphic Communications, Ottawa **Cover Illustration**: Gonzalo Millán (*Car and Couple*, 1975) **Production Coordination**: Patricio Ponce, Grafico, Montreal **Typography**: Set in Walbaum Standard by David Berman Typographics Ltd., Ottawa **Text Illustrations**: Gonzalo Millán.

The quote on page 50 is from Czeslaw Milosz's translation of "Report from a Besieged City" by Zbigniew Herbert, *The New York Review of Books*, No. 13, 1983

Printed and bound in Canada

The publisher gratefully acknowledges the assistance of the Ontario Arts Council.

Split Quotation
L'Esplanade Postal Outlet
P.O. Box 71037
Ottawa, Ontario
K2P 2L9

Contents

Introduction

Gonzalo Millán first appeared on the horizon of Chilean letters with *Relación Personal* (Santiago, 1968), a book that immediately won him a respected place among his generation. In this essentially lyrical poetry a minimized Self faces its options. Succinctness of expression and powerfully resonant images characterize this book, in which a certain objectivist tendency already begins to appear.

In *La ciudad*, published in Montreal in 1979, Millán's text resorts to experimental and self-referential techniques; in his most recent book, *Virus* (Santiago, 1987), the latter become the main theme. *Seudónimos de la muerte*, published in Chile in 1984, deals with the experience of exile and with life under an oppressive, repressive dictatorship.

La ciudad relates how the human and social order as well as the cosmic order and nature were destroyed by the military coup of 1973. The analysis of this destruction in an urban space that is both ubiquitous and referential takes language, the poetic medium, into the realm of meta-poetry; at the same time, however, it is a specific examination of the Spanish language, with a hint of parody of North American language text books. But this book is also important in another sense. In Chile after the coup in 1973, and among Chilean writers in exile, the literature of political commitment and denunciation has generally developed quite separately from the search for experimental or meta-poetic forms of expression. *La ciudad* achieved a perfect balance of theme and form and thus became one of the most important books in contemporary Chilean poetry.

Perhaps it is this combination of consummate craftsmanship and human perceptivity in Gonzalo Millán's poetry that has allowed him to play a leading role in Chilean poetry for the last two decades. His path begins by recasting and minimizing the inflated Self of Post-Surrealism, by redeeming objectivity and introducing colloquial language; it continues with the inescapable confrontation with the themes of coup and exile, both in their historical and human, intimate dimensions. This is shown through incidents of daily life and the alienation of everyday objects (*Vida*, Ottawa, 1984), through the experience of repression (*Seudónimos de la muerte*) and metapoetic reflection (*Virus*).

What follows from all this may sound like a cliché, but is perhaps the main reason for publishing this English edition of Millán's Selected Poems. Although these poems were produced in the context of Chile and exile and refer to it, they readily take on a universal dimension, thus meeting the basic test of any self-respecting lyricism, since only the shared Self can be truly individual. What inhabitant of a Canadian or Western city cannot identify with "The Object" and its implied epistemiology/ontology, the rule of habit that masks the alienation of daily life: "Triumphantly I say to the object/I desire: Now your are mine./The impenetrable object objects/ opaquely: You buy me,/but you have not paid for my secret".

But Gonzalo Millán is also active in other areas, such as visual poetry, samples of which the reader will find in this book and on the cover. His critical work includes the most complete inventory of poetry in Chile since the Sixties, "Promociones poéticas emergentes: el espíritu del valle" (Emerging Generations of Poets: The Spirit of the Valley), published in Concepción, Chile, in 1985. According to Millán, who takes a Taoist approach here, the Spirit of the Valley unites opposites and would serve as a guiding principle for a comprehensive "Chinese" anthology of the "emerging generations" of Chilean poets, regardless of antagonisms or groups among them. As a founding member of Ediciones Cordillera, the Chilean publishing house in Canada, and as editor in chief of

El espíritu del valle, the Chilean poetry magazine which was published jointly by Ediciones Cordillera and Casa Canadá in Chile from 1985 to 1988, Millán followed that philosophy, proving at the same time that nothing in poetry is foreign to him, the editor's role included.

In conclusion something else should be mentioned that the reader may already have noticed. Millán spent a significant part of his exile in Canada – New Brunswick, Ontario and Quebec – where, measured by the exacting standards applied to poetry in Chile, he produced texts of capital significance. He was involved in all of the major Chilean cultural initiatives in Canada. *La ciudad* was published in Montreal by Les Editions Maison Culturelle Québec-Amérique Latine in 1979; it is perhaps the most important book ever published in Spanish in Quebec. *Vida*, a collection of his work in Spanish, was published by Ediciones Cordillera in Ottawa in 1984; both books found a broad echo in Chile. We believe that this collection of poems in English will belatedly do justice to a body of work that was largely produced in Canada; its artistic skill and human universality call for its dissemination in this country.

Jorge Etcheverry

Translator's Foreword

My first attempts to translate some of these poems date back to the late seventies, shortly after they were written. My translations found their way to the occasional poetry reading – Harbourfront in Toronto, Gallery 101, ARC, Sasquatch in Ottawa – and a few were published here and there. But then the work came to a complete and full stop, after a battle with the author over the sex of death (see "Hockey", p. 187). I decided then that I could not afford any more such victories.

Some fifteen years later, with the author an Ocean away, and encouraged by an Ontario Arts Council grant and a supportive publisher, I began once more. Translating poetry is like reproducing Picasso's Blue Period in red. No wonder the author frets. I often asked myself, as the work proceeded, why I hadn't chosen a *dead* author instead, someone whose work was in the public domain and who, at worst, would turn over in his grave a few times. But in the end the author became accustomed to the strange new colour of his work. He was most helpful with clarifications of obscure *chilenismos* and with many constructive suggestions. It was reassuring to know that he would prevent major treason and live gracefully with the many minor betrayals that come with a translator's territory.

The title and structure of the book, the illustrations and the poems were chosen jointly by the author and myself. It was decided to include a representative sample from each of Millán's five published books. *The Teenager's Story* corresponds to *Relación Personal* (Arancibia Hermanos, Santiago, 1968), Millán's early work, written during his teenage years in Chile. When it appeared in 1968, it rceived an award as the best book of poetry published that year. *The Everyday House* was taken from the first part of *Vida* (Ediciones Cordillera, Ottawa, 1984); the second part of *Vida* appears towards the end of this book, as *A Strange House*. *Vae Victis* and 49th Parallel are parts I and II of *Seudónimos de la muerte* (Ediciones Manieristas, Santiago, 1984); *Virus* (Ediciones Ganymedes, Santiago, 1987) appears here under its original title: it is the book of the collapse of poetry, the crumbling of language. Millán himself supplied the translation of "Nickname"; it was only slightly modified by me.

The centrepiece of the book is *The City* (*La ciudad*, Les Editions Maison Culturelle Québec-Amérique Latine, Montreal, 1979). This long poem is quite untranslatable, and the text I finally produced is really an adaptation. I decided to work with a technique of substitution of images in order to preserve the tone of this magnificent long poem, rather than the literal meaning of each verse. *The City* is almost complete and for purposes of transparency it was decided to maintain the numbering of the original Spanish edition.

Millán writes in Spanish, the language of Cervantes and Nobel Prize winners, Gabriela Mistral, Pablo Neruda (both Chileans) and Octavio Paz. He builds up on one of the richest and most highly developed literary traditions in the world. During the seventies and early eighties he belonged to a group of Chilean writers in Canada that, with the generous support of the Canadian government, was able to make a significant contribution to the literature of Chile. Nevertheless Canadians tend to think of the "ethnic writer" – anyone who does not write in either English or French – as an amateur, qualitatively no different from someone performing a folk dance. I am pleased to present these Selected Poems by Gonzalo Millán to an English-speaking public, and I hope that my work will strike another nail into the coffin of the concept of the "ethnic writer".

My thanks go to Gonzalo Millán for his confidence, to Jorge Etcheverry, the publisher, for his encouragement and support, to all those who read, reviewed and commented on the translation, in particular Juan O'Neill who did a very thorough critical reading and also contributed much valuable editorial comment, and to the Ontario Arts Council for its translation grant.

Annegret Nill

Foreword to the English Edition

I am not the first member of my family to have gone into exile, and I probably won't be the last. In the 19th century the wars for the independence of Chile took one Antonio Millán to Argentina. During one of the civil wars with which the century closed (1891) my great-grandfather ended up living in Peru for some years. In this century several other relatives found themselves banished to Easter Island and Robinson Crusoe Island off the Pacific coast. I myself was forced by recent history to leave my country, first for Costa Rica in 1973, and then for Canada where I lived from 1974 to 1984.

Although I have deep roots in Chile, I agree with G.E. Lessing that any slight of the fatherland contains the beginnings of a virtue, especially now at the close of the 20th century where we see once more a resurgence of belligerent nationalisms. Perhaps the concrete and particular is preferable to those abstract concepts. To clarify my identity once and for all, I would say that today I am more Canadian than my father and brothers and sisters who never left Chile, and less Canadian than my daughter who grew up in Canada.

Now that the four books I wrote in Canada, far from their Spanish-speaking readers, have been published in Spanish, the English edition of my Selected Poems allows me to regain the public that was physically near at the time, but much more remote and unreachable than my Chilean readers.

My life here felt stagnant at times, like those closed locks in the Rideau Canal before an endless winter. But since then the locks have been raised and lowered many times and much water has flown through them, and as on a return to Santiago, Concepción or Arauco, my pulse speeds up when I walk past the strange houses along unforgettable streets in Fredericton, Montreal or Ottawa.

Gonzalo Millán

STRANGE HOUSES

Terror in the house does roar,
But Pity stands before the door.

William Blake

To the True Goddess

I.

The Everyday House

1. The Teenager's Story

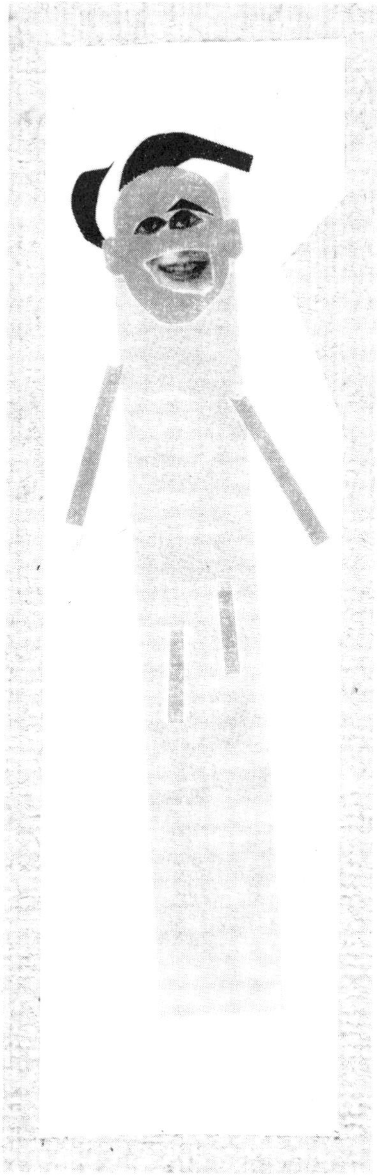

Self-Portrait of the Artist as a Young Man, 1979
Tapes on Canvas

Tale of the Fat White Kid and the Locust

Sitting under the curve of noon
I rub an insect between my fingers,
but suddenly a smile
escapes from my mouth
when I see the feet and wings
my nails tear out
fly from my bare hands
to the dust below.

We Travel in White Chariots

Hidden among the roots
stained by fruit peel and smoke
from burning leaves and paper,
I feel the blond
girlish silkiness of your legs
and, stiffening in my dirty hands,
the blue antler of my veins.

With a pebble you crack
the peach pit,
you chew the bitter seed
and throw it, sweetened, into my mouth.

I moisten a finger
and trace with saliva
the initials of your name on my thigh.
You throw dirt on them.
Dust falls afterwards.

I Play Children's Songs with a Grimace on My Lips

A broken doll buried in a garden
and cherries losing their sour taste in the water.
Behind the worm-eaten lances of a fence
petals stick to the lips
of a boy who is biting red flowers.
And I with my big hands begin
to play the toy piano from afar.

The Face of God

In one hand the black
and buttered stone,
sparkling in the fingers
of the awed child;
bitten, unappreciated,
the bread in the other hand.

The Mutilation of the Patios

From the lemon tree's new branch
dangle a pair of bird's feet,
dried and bound with a dirty cord.
No sign of the branch with the swing
or the languorous Castilian hen
that used to peck green pieces of glass.
Only a pile of sawdust and splinters.

Primal Scene

In the humid silence after
the cloudburst and thunder
the black bulb
of a rubber horn
squeezed by a child
interrogating the mystery.

The Sea and Your Underarm

The bold darkness
in the fold of your arm,
and snails sizzling
on the burning sand.

I looked at your underarm,
amazingly white,
then at the sea,
amazingly blue,
and reflected silently:

Today in the bathroom I saw
a razor dirty with hairs,
and in the wet sand
a decaying fish.

Your underarm, amazingly white:
the sea, amazingly blue.
Green algae, rotting
among the rocks.

My Hand No Longer Moves Blue Under the Water

Summer is slipping away from me
and the nude girl
with strings of seeds around her neck
gathering beach peas
in the sand.

I hear you now prowling around my house
and knocking on the door,
in a wool dress covered
with raindrops
and bits of bark.

You need not enter.
The dead summer's symbols
are beside you:
there is the feather of a bird
on the egg yolk,
and the sunflower head,
dry now,
is pinned to its stem.

An Extraordinary Guy

She was small and blonde
and had no breasts to speak of.
I am an extraordinary man
and had to go to sea,
work
and see the world.
Now she belongs to some poor guy.
I am an extraordinary man.
I saw the world,
I drank in the ports
and worked on a ship.
She was small and blonde
and had no breasts to speak of…

If You Opened My Fist, You Would Find My Palm Dirty

You know my eyes and on my mouth you know
the childish number of moles.
You know my crooked smile
and apart from that you know
that I lift one shoulder when I walk.
You only need to turn
the smooth and sun-drenched side of the stone
to see my other face,
buried in the earth.

Golden Record

I am pretending to play a guitar
with the hands that write,
and with the mouth that hums
these inaudible words
I am pretending to sing to a star-struck crowd
crazy to hear me.
I write this poem
like any boy
who composes a song
and knows that he will never be
among the top ten,
dreaming of the Nobel Prize
or the Golden Record.

Clinical Bulletin

Hour after hour every day
in foamy orange urine
I expel the rotten little eggs
and the worm I bit from your apple:
Queen of Armoured Hearts, fingered
and spattered playing card
from a second-hand deck.

I Limp Because You Limp. Forgive Me.

The ugly scar on your thin thigh
displeases me and seeing you
walk alone through the streets
makes me hide
behind newsstands
or turn to look at other women.
But when I cannot find your smell
or your hair on the pillow
I take this left sock
into my arms and this strange boot.

The Iron Tricycle Rims Without Tires and the Scratching of a Nail

We suddenly fall out of love
and are two bread crumbs
floating in a bowl of water,
or wingless flies,
chased by a finger across the table.
I remove your old lock
curled around my ear
and in our mouths
the razor blades of hatred vibrate
until the stench of green water in the vases
makes us drop the sand
we were holding in our hands
to throw into each other's eyes
and open the window once more.

Tale of the Cat and the Water Bird

Reflected in windows and water
I strutted before you,
golden and innocent,
and I flapped my chestnut-coloured wings
of wet feathers and, wrapped in my long double tail
of veils and fans, I made foam:

A little fish, dead now,
stiff and dry on the floor
after your soft paw
swept the fishbowl from the table.

I Press the Wavy Ear of Nothingness to My Ear

Empty shell of earth and vines:
feeble funnel that contains
the locust clouds of noise
and the wave wall's silence
before the crash and fall;
dark rosette that at the spiral's end
holds the whole night
in the dark hollow of its fruit;
coil of saliva
which I endlessly unravel;
crackling limestone, dry leaf,
until the fleeting presence
of light remains in my eyes,
and a trace of dust
and fluff between my fingers.

2. The Everyday House

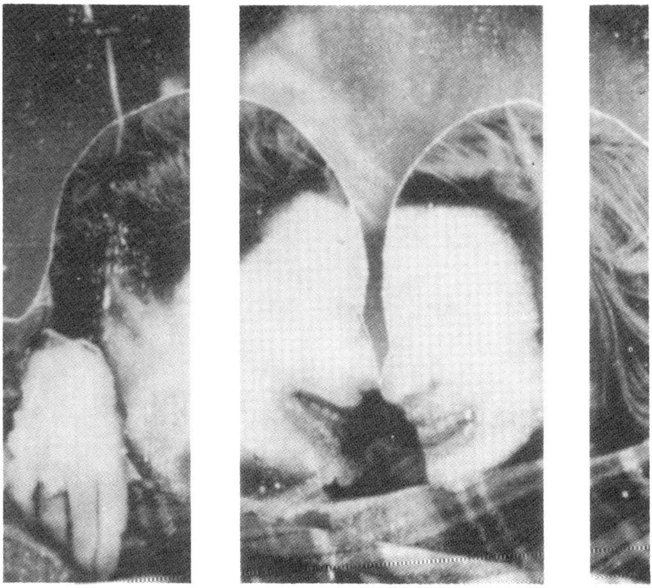

<u>Couple with Plaid</u>, 1979
Plastic Film

Le poème est toujours marié à quelqu'un.

René Char

Threshold

I don't envy my Master, decides
the shaggy Cerberus,
kicked out of hell
and chewing dice
on the threshold.

O'Connor Street Blues

I was no model husband
and even less a diplomat
like Rubens.

Nor was I loved
by celestial whores
or black saints.

Today I kiss neither
spiders nor bats,
nor the asses of mules
with angels' faces.

Older than yesterday
and younger than tomorrow,
alone and in peace,
I eat rice and beans
and drink my bitter green tea.

On Your Importance to Me Like an Ocean

Je ne te parlerais pas d'amour, je te parlerais seulement du temps qu'il fait.

Victor Chklovski

The oceans are the principal source
of the water vapour contained in the air.
The winds blow over them
and carry it to the land.
If on their way
the winds warm up,
the vapour does not liquefy.
But if they cool down,
the vapour condenses
and turns into snow or rain.

Dating Agency

The unknown is undesirable. It
was Ovid who said: "Ignoti nulla cupido".
Send us as soon as possible and without obligation
some full-length photographs
with your curriculum and preferences.
We are the secretaries of your secrets
and will test you free of charge
on our electronic equipment,
the Manifester of Incompatibilities,
for instance, that croaks
when love fails at first sight.

The Contract

I for my part bring to this contract
my devoted and devouring disgrace,
a bottle of cloves
(aphrodisiacs)
and the fear of the fragility of it all.

Wedding Presents

After regaling us
to their heart's content, they put us
up in an apartment
like the small couple
on top of the wedding cake,
seven stories high
                    and whitewashed.
In return, they each demanded
a slice of our lives.

Nest

I am not boasting. I do for you
what the woodpecker does
for his mate:
make a nest in a rotten tree.

Flutist

At last you are coming,
naked under the raincoat
done up with a row
of black buttons
like the holes of a flute.

Forgive my clumsy mouth
and my amateurish hands,
anxious to play
as soon as possible and in any way I can
the melody of your body.

The Kiss

Despite the absolute imperative stop signal
another train proceeds through the danger sign
and advances at full speed on the track.
The locomotive weighing more than 20 tonnes
advances at 80 km per hour.

At the rear of the stopped train
a passenger smokes absent-mindedly.
A sleeping dog on the platform
lifts his ears, and pigeons fly.
A porter drops his luggage and runs,
screaming, waving his arms.

The smoker suddenly recognizes
the woman who, gigantically in step
with her speeding heart,
throws herself into his arms.

Then foreheads and cheekbones clash,
noses and cheeks rub against each other.
Lips are crushed, making teeth collide,
breaths, tears, saliva intermingle.
Voraciously opened mouths devour each other.
The kiss razes everything in its way.

Palette

With a thumb in your sex
you are the painter's palette;
the ochres, reds, pinks
of your convulsed nude
on canvas sheets.

Kamasutra

The vaccination scar will remain
and the mole on your neck and under your arm.
The stretch marks will remain
behind the breasts and on the skin
around your waist, under the navel.

But not the crescent,
the wild boar's bite, the broken cloud,
the tiger's claw, the coral and the gem.
Traces of the art
of my teeth and nails.

A Dialectic of the Armless

To love one another we can manage without
our missing hands,
caressing one another
with our toes and tongues;
and to procreate we embrace
with the arms we do not have.

Stork's Egg

I clearly see in an oval soap
the child's face taking shape.
Its face is covered with down.
Extremities end in hands.
Stellar pinpoints twinkle
in its lemur's eyes.
Its foamy features glove
my dirty hands giving birth.

Ablution

I have not seen
and might never see
a black otter
among white water lilies,
but it is beautiful to imagine,
as, for the armless,
to imagine soap
the colour of beets
between white foamy hands.

Branch

The everyday house
is a different house at this hour.
The shadow of the benign
branch is transfigured
and hurls itself through the window
like a panther's paw
pouncing on the cradle.

Fears

Sometimes
cats
have
puppies.

Incubator

1. Valve
2. Regulator
3. Thermostat
4. Deflector
5. Air Generator
6. Lamp
7. Box
8. Humidifier
9. Double wall
10. Double bottom
11. *Premature*

Like the First Time

You have not yet regained your figure.
There are stretch marks on your belly
and a contraceptive
needle prick on your buttock,
candy, clean sheets.

Naked and nervous like the first time,
after the birth of our child.

One can hear an empty truck rattle
through the flower-lined road on the hill
and then, striking the hour of love,
goldenrod shedding pollen.

Jewel

Your breasts are not ablaze
with strings of precious stones.
At most there dangles from your neck,
like a baroque teardrop,
a grain of yellow rice.

Rent

I kiss the rudiment of victory,
my daughter's infinitesimal fist,
and this time I am not writing verses,
scrawls, obscene epithets
on the wretched bills
before I pay the rent.

We live under the threat of a roof
that regularly brings us to our knees.

On a beach of discordant waves
we were catching octopi among the rocks
last summer, with grappling hooks,
and did they ever cling!

First Steps

The garden was an orchestra
tuning its instruments
until you appeared,
you with spring,
prodigious conductor, barely rising from the ground
and unsteadily grasping my finger.

A Happy Bedtime Story

Giants consist of numerous dwarfs
like the ears of grains.
Sometimes the terrible giants
feel tickled and laugh.
It's the dwarfs,
making grimaces in their skins
with their little faces.

Transitional Bear

I ask you what you are hiding
in your fist.
You keep silent.
But when sleep
half opens your fingers
I discover the treasure
that has cost
the teddybear
one of his eyes.

The Present

As one paper tissue
with its fold pulls
the next one from the box,
the days succeed one another.

Between the past and tomorrow
goes the present,
like a lame girl
on crutches.

Death follows her
like an agent,
leafing through the pages
of strange agendas.

E.T.

You are on the shore of another planet,
at the edge of a vast blue brine
where harmless animals roam
which they call seagulls and cats.

The seagulls have arms with feathers
and the fishes are covered with fingernails.

A female human throws garbage
through a window into the sea, red and green,
fish guts and lettuce
leaves. The cat babbles gibberish.

Everything whirrs, glistens and moves.
The sun radiates a vibrant strangeness.

Family

The clocks stopped and the people were
bereft of movement and voice.

Carlos Pellicer

The head of the household takes a few steps
in rigid trousers,
he moves his smiling face
from left to right
while his smiling wife
repeats a gesture with her arm
until the head of the household
stops at her side
and they embrace with a smile.

They watch how on a patch of grass
the children happily throw
a ball at a dog and the dog
with the ball in his muzzle runs
to deposit it at the children's feet
while all the time merrily wagging
his tail.

The clock strikes and its hands stop
instantly.
The mechanism is broken
and the family, motionless, smiles at us.

Vacation

Two couples come running out of the water.
They are laughing. There are
explosions around their ankles.

A blonde woman is in front.
She is wearing a one-piece swimsuit,
milky, brand name Catalina, and has
one leg, the left one, lifted up.

She is followed by a well-built bather
who is wearing black swimming trunks,
brand name Catalina, with a light-coloured belt,
and has one leg, the left one, in the air.
With one hand he reaches back
towards a brunette with a damp
swimsuit which looks like silver in the sun.
The V of her neckline shows off her cleavage.

She is followed by a man who stumbles
as he runs in purple bathing trunks.

Laughing and motionless they come running
    out of the water.

The waves of the sea make foam
when they smash into the cliffs.

Hermit

You whom reverend love made one another's hermitage.

John Donne

Go join a convent
or lock yourself up in a cave!
my wife screams at me.
What for, if the house
is the convent,
its altars the kitchen,
the bathroom, our bodies,
the bed and the table?
What for, when like the cave and the hermit
we are made for one another?

Yellow Apples

I would gladly live in the refrigerator
if you did not love me,
like a hermit at the Pole,
nourished only by the aroma
of yellow apples.

Triptych

In the foreground a couple
is removing something
from an overflowing refrigerator.
The open door copies,
like the second panel of a diptych, the shelves
of a mini-supermarket.
Black and white checkered floor tiles.
On the threshold at the end of the hallway
a messenger is delivering a telegram.

Outside a jet,
a lawnmower and an automobile.
Inside a dishwasher
and a running vacuum cleaner.
They groan and roar.

Around the corner
the butcher is reading a blood-stained paper
while soldiers are marching through the street.
A woman with only one breast
looks at herself naked in the mirror.
The milkman tilts a bottle of wine.
The man with TB spits into the well.
A child walks through the square
and leaves in the beggar's hand
a button with an anchor and three holes.

Plate

In the amphitheatre, ruins;
remnants of toppled columns.
And on the plate, fishbones,
vertebrae of sardines.

The Bridge

This bridge that once united us,
the refectory table,
is now closed off by an unsurmountable
barrier of platters,
plates, glasses and bottles.
We eye one another, wielding
threatening eating utensils
from distant banks,
while under the table
our feet between the rigid
kneeless legs
grope in vain,
wanting to ford the current that separates us.

A Dog's Life

The tomcats stalk
through the withering weeds
of the garden rank
with exhaust gases;
they jump their females
and pant and screech
on top of them.

Then they come in
for their bowls of milk;
with slow licks
they clean their furs;
they walk along walls
or roll in rags.

I spend much time
stroking their backs
and I envy them nine times.

Truce

Today there are no field reports,
all is quiet on the personal front.
Nor are there clinical bulletins
or love letters or bills.

The menu of the day, frugal.
The weather, rather temperate.
A white butterfly appears,
a fluttering banner of truce.

Fur Coat

We were vivacious otters,
jubilant rivals,
frolicking untiringly
in a mirror of water.

Reminiscing, the sun
has a luster of varnish
or artificial tears,
now that the twin skins
make up an unused coat
hanging in a closet.

Reflections

My eyes are no longer enough
to corroborate your beauty.
You search in the streets
for alien mirrors, other eyes
—the head of a nail
is a minute moon.
You contemplate
        a can of sardines
        filled with rainwater.

Relics

To think that only yesterday
we were like cherries joined
over a child's ear,
years which now
seem just like summer afternoons.

The Wrecker

We were sleeping embraced
like two drops of water
when we were awakened
by knocking on the door
of the old house.
I am the wrecker, said
a stranger,
smiling at my wife,
and came in to lie down
between us
upside down
in the middle of the bed.

Repairs

You hear the board that always creaks
when you step on the threshold of sleep.
Tomorrow you will nail it without fail,
striking burned matches
like feeble nails,
with a hammer that goes up in smoke.

The Demolition

I wake up in the middle of the night
from the noise of hammer blows.
They are about to demolish the house,
and the furtive wreckers
mask their banging
with my heartbeat.

Domestic Apocalypse

The sheets that had been wedding presents
are torn and threadbare now.
The dishes were smashed
in domestic skirmishes.
The cups are cracked, they have lost their handles.
The forks are lost and stained
the stainless knives.
The pitcher is broken.
And the diamond ring is in the pawnshop.
On the calender
all the days have been crossed off.
The clock has wound down.
The tea has run out, the coffee, the bread,
the butter.
All that's left is a few drops of oil.
Empty eggshells.
In the refrigerator there is only
half a dehydrated onion
and a baby bottle with sour milk.
A mouse hiding in its hole
gnaws on what's left of a cube of sugar.
The furnace went out last night
after using up its fuel.
The telephone has been cut off, and soon
they'll cut the light.
Three or four lightbulbs are still
working in the house.
The candles have burned down to stumps.

The toilet paper has run out
and the toilet is clogged
with pieces of newsprint.
The soap will vanish
next time someone washes his hands.
The comb has lost another tooth.
The splinter in the mirror is yet another wrinkle.
There is no clean laundry left.
The bathtub is full of dirty diapers.
The shirt has lost its last
remaining button.
On top of the table,
small fingerprints,
bibs, dirty dishes
with crumbs and fishbones.
Glasses with dried purple crusts.
Curled up in the empty fruit bowl
sleeps the cat.
The old car parked outside
has not started in months or years.
Immobile it rests on its axles,
on piles of pebbles and bricks.
They have stolen the tires, the headlights,
and every day they strip it of more parts,
like a large dead insect
being devoured by invisible ants.
The garden is vigorous and luxuriant,
overgrown with weeds that smother the flowers.

The slithering gardenhose is invisible.
The canary has fled from its cage,
and the goldfish is floating belly up
in the muddy water of its tank.
The dog has chewed through the leash
and has left in pursuit of a bitch.
The milkman no longer delivers milk to the house
nor is the paper boy bringing the paper.
The letter carrier brings only unpaid bills.
Envelopes with windows which no one opens.
The creditors knock for a long time,
but no one opens, no one responds.
The garbage is picked up twice a week,
but too early in the morning.
In the yard the garbage cans are flowing over,
they stink.
The TV has no sound
and throws moving shadows
on the floor powdered
with plaster dust
raining from the ceiling.
A child in a wooden playpen,
surrounded by toys, cries at the top of his voice,
hungry and wet,
his moist mouth open,
his eyes glassy with tears
watching
how the double-backed beast
growls and writhes convulsively,
attempting to devour itself.

II.

The City

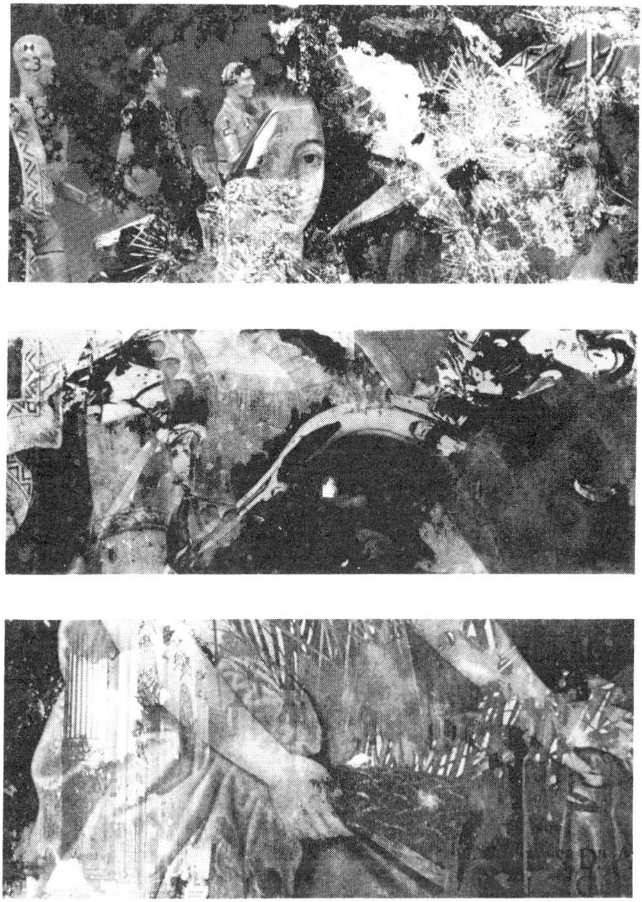

Doña Josefa Guzmán, (after Gil de Castro), 1976
Plastic Film

And even if the City falls and one of us survives
he will carry the City inside him on the roads of exile
he will be the City

we look at the face of hunger the face of fire the face of death
and the worst of them all—the face of treason
and only our dreams have not been humiliated

Zbigniew Herbert

1.

Sunrise.
The poem opens.
The birds open their wings.
The birds open their beaks.
Roosters crow.
Flowers open.
Eyes open.
Ears open.
The city awakens.
The city rises.
Taps are opened.
Water runs.
Razors scissors are opened.
Bolts curtains are opened.
Doors letters are opened.
Newspapers are opened.
The wound breaks open.

Over the waters rises fog.
Tall buildings rise up.
Cranes raise heavy objects.
The winch raises the anchor.

Traffic flows in the streets.
Crowded buses run.
The buses stop.
Corner stores open.
Big department stores open.
Trains run.

The pen flows.
The writing flows fast.
Banks open their safes.
Customers withdraw deposit money.
Mud forms deposits.
Mud is deposited in stagnant waters.

Several bridges cross the river.
Trains cross the bridge.
Trains run on rails.
The bridge is made of iron.
Time runs.
The wind runs.
The trains clatter.

From the chimneys rises smoke.
The river flows fast.
Dirty water flows in the sewers.
The sewers empty into the river.
The water gurgles.
Hens cluck.
Cluck cluck say the hens.

The river is deep.
The river is wide.
Rivers have tributaries.
The tributaries have waterfalls.
The tributaries empty into the river.
Avenues are wide.
Streets empty into the avenue.
The river empties into the sea.
The sea is wide.

2.

Automobiles circulate.
Rumours of war circulate.
Money circulates.
Blood circulates.

Pedestrians go to work.
The pedestrians cross at the street corners.
The pedestrians circulate on the sidewalks.
The men wear pants.
The agents wear raincoats.
They place agents at the street corners.

Wretched men circulate.
The unemployed circulate.
Clouds hide the blue of the sky.
Clouds hide the light of the sun.
Clouds circulate at great altitudes.

Snow is white.
The condor flies at great altitudes.
There is snow at great altitudes.

3.

The watches go.
Planets go.
How is it going?
I go hungry.
I go penniless.
I go ragged.
I go dirty.
I go alone.
I go in fear.
I am going away.
I am too ill to go.
Begone! they said.
They are going after me.
I am going abroad.
It is tough going.
Let's go!
Good-bye.
The Andes are going white.

4.

The floodgates open.
The floodgates let the water pass.
Ambulances wail.
The cars let an ambulance pass.
Ambulances are white.
The amber light is bright.
The blinds are wide.
The eyes look at the blinds.
The pores let the sweat pass.
The sick man rests several hours a day.

Weekdays pass.
There was soccer.
There was tennis.
Today there is no work.
There are no vacancies.
The schoolchildren run.
Computers run.
Water runs through lead pipes.

They run tabs.
Those who resist run risks.
The cyclists run pursue one another.
The boats pursue schools of fish.
I am on the run they are pursuing me.
The persecutions help make converts.

Accounts are opened.
Soup opens the meal.
The forest is shady.
Trails open up in the forest.
The owl hoots.

Rabbits dig burrows.
The gravediggers dig a pit.
The prisoners dig a hole.

5.

Coaches are passing by.
Funerals pass through this street.
They have shot many.
The streets have many holes.
The horses wear black saddlecloths.
Hee! says the horse.
Trucks are passing by.
Cars of affluent men pass by.
Schoolchildren are passing by.
A dwarf with a big head passes by.
The tyrant passes by in an armoured car.

To pass over the abuse.
The shots late at night.
Not to open one's mouth except to eat.
When there is something to put in one's mouth.
We go hungry.
One cannot speak openly.
Parrots speak readily.
The parrot has colourful feathers.
Birds of a feather nest in the newsrooms.
Parrots speak on the radio.
The gag prevents speech.

Wr ggd.
Wre gged.
We’re ggged.
We are gagged.
We are blindfolded.
The eyes open under the blindfold.
The mouth opens under the gag.

The tyrant enjoys good health.
Only man enjoys the gift of speech.
The gorillas are drumming on their chests.
Death to the tyrant!

6.

Someone starts to run. They follow him.
The pedestrians make way.
They run around a corner.
The informer sneaks away stealthily.

To hide the rage.
To hide the disgust.
To hide the poverty.
To hide the hunger.
To bite one's tongue.
To act with great stealth.

7.

It is fall in the city.
The leaves are turning red.
The leaves are turning yellow.
The leaves are wilting.
The leaves are falling.
Fallen leaves are useless.
The junta does not fall.
The tyrant does not fall.

The wind blows.
The leaves fly.
The wind sweeps up the leaves.
Dry leaves whirl around.
There are whirlpools in the river.
Red leaves float in the river.
Leaflets are whirled up.
Birds whirl through the air.

The river follows its course.
Fall follows summer.
They follow in my footsteps.
The days become shorter.
April follows March.
They extend the curfew.
They extend the state of siege.
April has thirty days.
April is the fourth month of the year.
The days pass.
Another leaf falls from the calendar.

8.

The sun sets.
Water falls from the spout into the fountain.
The water cascades.
A cascade is the old man's voice.
The soldiers retreat.
Soldiers are housed in barracks.
Hotels house travellers.
The population retires early.
Hours before curfew.
Butterflies fly in the sunset.
The birds retire to their nests.
The sea covers the shore and retires.
The day is declining.
The street lights are turned on.
The city lights up.
Butterflies circle the light.
Strength declines with age.
Years of few lights.
These last years of mine.
We live in darkness.
The old man turns on the light.
Click! go the switches.
The rooms light up.
Television sets are turned on.
The tyrant speaks on all channels.
It gets dark early in winter.
The neon signs blink on and off.
The stores close.

The streets are emptying.
The first stars appear.
Pedestrians walk hastily.
The pedestrians hurry.
The first patrols appear.
Curfew begins.
The moon appears.

9.

The day has twenty-four hours.
The lighbulb is lit twenty-four hours.
The lightbulb hangs in the middle of the room.
The air in the room is heavy.
Doors and windows stay closed.
The prisoners sit with bent heads.
The prisoners are sitting on chairs.
The prisoners are blindfolded.
Brows and eyelashes stick to the blindfold.
The eyelids move under the blindfold.
The hands swell.
The hands are tied with ropes.
They take a hooded prisoner from the room.
The prisoners moan whisper move.
The prisoners must remain motionless.
The prisoners must remain silent.
Any violation is punished severely.
The prisoners receive food once a day.
The broth is thin and served cold.
The prisoners drink water by rations.
The prisoners are not allowed to wash themselves.
The prisoners go to the toilet once a day.
After midnight they are allowed to
stretch out on the floor.
The one who went for questioning
has not returned.
The prisoners sleep in their clothes.
At night they hear other prisoners scream.
The prisoners are wakened in the morning.

10.

The shopwindows are filled with dummies.
Dummies are made of plaster.
The dummies are motionless.
The dummies are elegant.
The dummies wear expensive clothes.
Brand new unused clothes.
The dummies are not cold.
The dummies are not hungry.
The dummies look healthly.
They are happy.
They are always smiling.

11.

The earth moves.
Teeth move before they fall out.
Children change teeth.
Baby teeth fall out.
Milk falls into a bucket.
The cow gives milk.
The bull charges.
The storm clouds are charged.
A drizzle falls.
The soldiers charge their rifles.
The busboys carry charged trays.
I have many children in my charge.
The burden is overwhelming.
We carry the weight of the dictatorship.
They exchange two potatoes for a
    handful of noodles.
They exchange half a loaf of bread for a bit of oil.
Changes in the cabinet.
They change the water in the vase.
Soldiers leave. Civilians enter.
Snakes change skins.
Red light.
The traffic lights change.
The chameleon changes colour.
The vehicles stop.
They change the sick man's sheets.
The mattress is stuffed with wool.

The sheets cover the mattress.
The shepherd watches the sheep.
The sheep give wool.
The beauty watches her figure.
The sick man watches the ceiling.
A mouse falls into the mousetrap.
The date falls to the foot of the date palm.

12.

The wind is shifting.
The wind announces rain.
The switchman shifts the switches.
The engine switches tracks.
The tender follows the engine.
The engine hauls cars.
The wind hauls leaves.
The weather is shifting.
The leaves are covered with frost.
The sky is covered with large clouds.
The clouds threaten rain.

The leaves take leave of the tree.
Tomorrow we leave the city.
They saw them leave at the airport.
The wind carries off the leaves.
It was a moving leave-taking.
Steam leaves the mouths.
A fragrant scent leaves the rose.
The rose reigns over the flowers.
The beauty reigns over women.
A putrid smell leaves the mud.
Misery reigns.
Unemployment reigns.
Fear reigns in the city.

There are no leaves on the trees.
Mushrooms have no leaves.
I asked for an advance.
I was asking for the moon.
Rain announces itself in advance.

The player asks for cards.
The fiancé asks for her hand.
It never rains but it pours.
The tyrant asks for sacrifices.
Winter has arrived.

13.

It rains.
Rain stains the streets.
Wet asphalt is shiny.
The pedestrians cover themselves.
The hat covers the head.
The umbrella protects from the rain.
Shoes slip into galoshes.
Galoshes are made of rubber.
The ball is made of rubber.
The ball bounces on the ground.
The rain bounces on the ground.
It rains buckets.
Buckets are for carrying water.
The rain-water forms puddles.
Mud forms in the puddles.
The rain forms bubbles when it hits the puddles.
Cars splash.
The water bounces off the roofs.
The roofs leak.
The rain drips into buckets.
The water runs off the roofs.
Eavestroughs collect the water.
The roofs drip.
Rain hits the windows.
The drops glide off the glass.

The rain soaks.
The rain dampens the walls.
The earth is soaked.
It rains in the city.
It rains in the poem.
The old man writes:
Raindrops aren't pennies.
If only raindrops were pennies.

14.

The walls are plumb.
The walls are high.
Walls close off.
Walls separate.

They gag the walls with paint.
The rain washes it off.
Fragments of murals appear.
And the last RESISTANCE just erased.

15.

The elevators go up.
Sales go down.
The elevator man is eager to help.
The elevators go down.
Informers are everywhere.
The elevator man is an informer.
The sick man's fever goes up.
Prices go up.
The price of copper goes down.
The tide rises.
The waters of the river rise.
The waves rise upstream.
The current clashes with the tide.
The miners go down into the mine.
The preacher goes up to the pulpit.
The deceased goes down to the grave.

The curtain rises.
The actor goes up to the stage.
The actor plays a role.
The roll of paper is white.
The performance is interrupted.
They evacuate the room.
They arrest several actors.
The police have broad powers.

They dismiss several generals.
The passengers go on deck.
They dismiss thousands of workers.

The buses stop.
Passengers get off the buses.
Passengers board the bus.
They pay sit down.
The cable car goes up.
The cable car goes down.
The landing gear goes down.
The airplane lands.
Passengers get off the airplane.
The airplanes land take off.
Cattle graze under the airplanes.
The train stops.
Travellers get off the train.
Porters carry luggage.
The identity card carries a photograph.
They ask for identification.
They arrest those without papers.
A pedestrian's heart stops.
The pedestrian suffers a cardiac arrest.
Plop! he drops dead in the street.

The businessmen take measures.
The seamstress takes measurements.
The seamstress takes the needle.
The old man picks up the pen.
Ink flows to the pen.
Blood flows to the heart.
The pen scrapes over the paper.
The soles scrape the soil.
The pen draws slanted strokes.

The blind man strikes the chords.
The beauty has slanted eyes.
The beauty applies make-up to her eyes.
The beauty carries her head high.
Vehicles carry licence plates.
They take down the licence number.
The sick man has been in bed for months.
They take the sick man's pulse.
The pulse is intermittent.
They take tea.
They take coffee.
The drunks take wine.
The fuel gauges go down.
The fuel gauges go up.
The sick man's fever goes down.
The flag goes up the mast.
The tide goes down.
The flag waves.
The waves ebb and flow.
Hair waves in the wind.
The beauty waves her hair.
The snake moves in waves.

The waves go up down.
The river has waves.
The temperature goes down.
The gate goes down at the railway crossing.

16.

The earth is round.
The table is round.
The table is made of wood.
They set the table.
The tablecloth covers the wood.
The table is set.
The place settings are on the tablecloth.
The place setting consists of
Knife.
The knife has a handle and a blade.
The knife cuts.
Spoon.
The spoon is concave.
You eat soup with the spoon.
Fork.
The fork has prongs.
The fork pricks.
Glass.
The glass contains water.
The glass is made of quartz.
Bread.
The bread is in the bread basket.
The bread has crust and crumb.
The crumb is soft.
The bread basket is made of straw.
Napkin.
The napkin cleans the lips.
The napkin is white.

The table has four legs.
The legs are round.
The chairs have four legs.
The chairs surround the table.
The chairs have no armrests.
The children bring the chairs close.
The family sits down at the table.
On the table are soup plates.
The hands grip the spoons.
They serve soup with the ladle.
Bread is broken with the fingers.
The toasted crust cracks.
Crumbs fly.
Crumbs cover the tablecloth.
The teeth bite into the bread.
Man has thirty-two teeth.
Eight incisors.
Four canines.
Twenty molars.
The teeth grind the food.
The food falls into the stomach.
The stomachs are not full.
The family eats in silence.
The family is incomplete.
It rains outside.

17.

The sun comes out.
The residents come out of their houses.
It is cold.
The square is wide and without houses.
The men raise their collars.
The birds raise their wings.
The women wrap themselves in scarves.
The street comes from the square.
No jobs are coming up.
The unemployed come out hungry.
There are no vacancies.
Too many arms are idle.

The school children go back to school.
He goes out to make a phone call.
He enters a phone booth.
The phones are tapped.
Ring! goes the telephone.
The schools are infiltrated.
They raise the food prices.
They raise the bus fares.
Plainclothes agents stop them.
The detainees raise their arms.
Those who are cold stamp their feet.
Those who are cold blow into their hands.
The scarf covers the neck.
Gloves cover the hands.
The schoolchildren come out for recess.

The guard comes out of the guardhouse.
The children slide over the frozen surface.
Wheels skid.
The funeral procession enters the cemetery.
A boat leaves port.
Smoke leaves the nose.
The smokers leave butts.
Beggars gather them up.
They pick up stray dogs.
They pick up garbage.
They pick up letters at the mailbox.
The beauty gathers up her hair.
The beauty steps out on the balcony.
The beauty goes shopping.
The beauty covers herself well.
They cover the sick man well.
The sick man enters the operating room.
The surgeon operates.
The surgeon cuts with the knife.
The cold cuts the hands.
The cold cuts the skin.
With the cold come chilblains.
The sick man leaves the operating room.
Chilblains burn itch.
Fire protects from the cold.
The lawyer defends the accused.
The official slaps the lawyer.
Bellows fan the fire.
They laugh in his face.
They cut his argument to pieces.

Bars defend the windows.
Client and lawyer disappear.
The breakwater fends off the waves.
The rain freezes.
Hail falls.
They throw thousands into the street.
They throw coal into the brazier.
They throw firewood into the fireplace.
The firewood does not burn.
They throw paraffin into the stove.
The firewood is wet.
They catch a messenger.
They catch extremists.
The beauty catches cold.
Warm water circulates.
The radiators spread heat.

The cold cracks the lips.
The cold causes hoarseness.
The teeth chatter.
The cold cracks the skin.

It is extremely cold in the street.
Misery is extreme.
The cold turns people blue.
We are having the blues.
The cold burns the plants.
They left us planted in the street.
The cold contracts bodies.

The cold contracts muscles.
The cold freezes puddles.
Meat is kept frozen.
The meat hangs from the hook.
They hang up dead animals.
After death the muscles contract.
The cold delays putrefaction.

18.

She distracts herself looking out of the window.
The window overlooks the street.
The street is deserted.
It rains cats and dogs.
That house is bigger than this one.
This house is smaller than that one.
Opposite the window is the church.
In the church there is a wedding.
It is imprudent to ring the bells
        during a thunderstorm.
The rain soaked her dress.
The groom got soaked to the skin.
It was a happy union.

19.

It rains oceans.
Hot water boils.
Water boils at 100°.
The sea is boiling.
The sea is rough.
The tortured howl.
The sea howls.
The wind howls between the trees.
The sea rages.
The sea lashes the rocks.
The prisoners receive lashes.
Violent winds lash the coast.
Majestic waves rise up.
The wind curls the waves.
A waterspout rises from the sea.
The waterspout spins.

Lightning lights up the sky.
A man was struck by lightning.
Lightning moves snake-like.
Thunder.
The thunder has an echo.
Thunder goes with lightning.
Milk curdles in thunderstorms.
Telephone wires are cut.
Eggs become addled in the thunderstorm.

The wind picks up speed.
The wind runs behind garbage cans.
The river has a strong current.
An automobile ran over a pedestrian.
The thread runs off the spool.
Trees protect from the wind.
The wind delays the march.
The return to normal is delayed.
The bus is delayed.
The trains are delayed.
A landslide has buried the railway tracks.
Flights are cancelled.
The airplanes are grounded.
The lion roars.
The storm roars.
Lightning strikes the lightning rod.
Lightning splits the wood.
An avalanche of stone and mud falls.
Traffic gets bogged down on the roads.
The gale lifts off roofs.
The gale blows off the tar paper.
Tar paper and boards fly.
Wind and water take their toll.
Rain leaks between the boards.
Wind leaks through.
Rain floods the slums.
Puddles form in the rooms.
Beds float.
The firemen and police are mobilized.
The jobless form cleanup crews.

The cold gets worse.
A special envoy arrives.
There is extreme vigilance.
They administer extreme unction to the sick man.
The river grows impetuously.
The river overflows its bed.
The river floods the fields.
It covers the countryside with water.
The orchards were flooded.
A dam burst.
The suburbs are under water.

20.

A torrential rain falls.
The rain swells the torrents.
The torrents cause floods.
Today there is a benefit performance
for the flood victims.
Rain is indispensable for agriculture.
Rain fertilizes the earth.
Wheat germinates in spring.
The ears of wheat contain grains.
The plough gets caught in the roots.
Oxen are put before the plough.
The peasant goads on the oxen.
Wheat is scarce this year.
The passage of the troops destroyed the crops.
The rats ravage the granaries.
The weeds impoverish the fields.
Money is scarce.
I have scarcely a handful of flour.
Bread prices rise.
We live with scarcity.
Food is scarce.
Work is scarce.
The unemployed are abundant.
Oil is scarce.
Water is abundant.
Oil is thicker than water.
Oil hardens when it is cold.
Oil penetrates the fabrics.
The sword penetrates the flesh.
The sword has a pointed end.

22.

Daybreak.
The waves break forming whitecaps.
Mass lay-offs follow each other.
The waves follow each other.
The waves of the sea break.
The boat breaks the waves.
The waves break on the rocks.
There are rocks in the middle of the sea.
Rumours are afloat.
Boats are afloat.
They import bundles of used clothing.
The boats dock at the pier.
The pier reaches into the sea.
The bay reaches into the shore.
Ships ride at anchor in the bay.
There are dunes on the coast.
The sand dunes advance.
Pine groves detain the dunes.
The cape advances into the sea.
The rain stops.
They detain citizens.
The vehicles stop.
Green light.
The detentions continue.
The pine tree is an evergreen.
A bird flies into the pine tree.
Floodgates stop the water.
From the pine tree flows turpentine.
The tide flows back.

23.

Logs float down the river.
The wood piles up in the sawmill.
The saw shows teeth.
The saw no longer cuts wood.
The plane has a blade.
The plane no longer planes wood.
The hammer no longer strikes the nail.
The carpenter sold the saw.
                    Sold the plane.
                    Sold the hammer.
The carpenter has no work.
No one is building any more.
The wood piles up in the sawmill.
The woodborer eats away the wood.

24.

The key enters the lock.
The fingers enter the gauntlet.
The key turns.
The photographer enters the darkroom.
The tamer enters the cage.
The couple enters the honeymoon suite.
Whoosh! goes the whip.
The prisoner enters the torture suite.
The wild beasts jump.
The nail enters the wall.
All circuses have clowns.
But none like the tyrant.
They uncover the pots.
The sick man uncovers himself.
The cork covers the bottle.
The bottle contains wine.
The wine comes out of the bottle.
Gluglu! goes the wine.
The drunks enter the bar.
An airplane enters into a tailspin.
The wine is going sour.
The ship enters drydock.
The sea is rough.
The soldiers close ranks.
The schoolchildren close ranks.
An officer harangues them.
The schoolchildren salute the flag.
The flag is hoisted on the flagpole.
They intone the national anthem.

25.

She appeared.
She had disappeared.
Months later she appeared.
They found her.
They found her with a wire around her neck.
They found her on a beach with a wire
    around her neck.
They found here on a beach.
With her backbone broken and a wire
    around her neck.

26.

The clock strikes twelve.
They give medicine to the sick man.
The medicine is bitter.
The medicine is necessary.
Pontificate government economists.
They express their sympathy to the widow.
They kick the dog.
The dog howls.
They slam the door in the beggar's face.
The house has a front door.
The tycoon counts money in front of the beggar.
Thanks for nothing.
The house overlooks the garden.
The garden has marble statues.
The walnut tree gives walnuts.
A walnut hits the ground.
Walnuts have hard shells.
Unemployment is hard.
The walnut splits in two.
A train departs.
They split wood.
The last refugees depart.
They give the sick man something to calm him.
The sea calms itself.
The thunderstorm calms itself.
The wind abates.
The weather has cleared up.
The situation continues to be stormy.
The repression does not abate.

27.

I descend from illustrious grandparents.
I have numerous descendants.
I obey the commandments.
I give work to thousands of workers.
I give my arm to my wife.
I give an education to my children.
I give alms to the poor.
I give my support to the government.
I give a constitution to the country.
I live in a residential neighbourhood.
I have a house with servants.
I have a driver in uniform.
I have a butler with livery.
I have maids with caps.
The maid waits at table.
The soldiers use uniforms.
The soldiers serve the country.

I mix with persons of my standing.
I mix work with holidays.
Clear days are mixed with rainy ones.
I am of clear ancestry.
The eggwhite is clear and liquid.
The eggwhite is somewhat salty.
Blood is somewhat salty.
Definitions must be clear and brief.

28.

It is clearing up.
Cock-a-doodle-doo! crow the cocks.
The sun cheers up the streets.
The sick man takes heart.
The cockscomb is red.
The eaves drip.
The sparrows flutter.
The sparrows nest in the eaves.
The sunlight is bright.
Babies see the light.
Another mouth to feed.
The mother coos to her child.
Pigeons coo.
Pigeons nest in the roof.
The sun scatters the clouds.
Time scatters illusions.
The wind sweeps the clouds from the sky.
They sweep the snow from the railway tracks.
The wind leaves the trees in peace.
The weather has cleared up.
The lawn is wet with dew.
Dew falls in the morning.
The diamond is pure and hard.

The sun sends out beams.
The sunbeams turns dew into diamonds.
The streets become animated.
The city becomes animated.
The sea shimmers.
The sun glistens on the river.
The brilliance of the sun is incomparable.

30.

They disavowed the authorities.
They disdained the constitution.
They dismantled the presidential palace.
They defaced the parks.
They defiled the sidewalks.
They dislodged the nails.
They dislocated bones.
They debranched the bushes.
They debudded the branches.
They discased the swords.
They discomforted the grieving.
They disconnected the wires.
They deflated the balloons.
They defoliated the forests.
They deforested the hills.
They disrooted the seedlings.
They demagnetized the compasses.
They desilverized the money.
They devitrified the windows.
They devocalized the singers.
They dispensed with formalities.
They dehorned the bulls.
They disentombed the dead.
They dismasted the ships.
They dismembered the territory.
They dismissed the complaints.
They demoralized the youth.
They denationalized the mines.

They denaturalized the citizens.
They denatured the milk.
They denitrified the air.
They denuded the orphans.
They decalcified the bones.
They decapitated the statues.
They deglutinated the flour.
They dehydrated the children.
They deoxygenated the blood.
They discoloured the furniture.
They disfurnished the rooms.
They discomfitted the residents.
They disconcerted the orchestras.
They defrauded the public.
They defrocked the priests.
They defrosted the freezers.
They degassed the street lights.
They degummed the stamps.
They deiced the glaciers.
They deified themselves.
They displanted the crops.
They detached the roofs.
They disdained the inhabitants.
They disbarred the lawyers.
They disbanded the courts.
They disembowelled the cattle.
They despoiled the libraries.
They demolished the books.
They depleted the museums.
They decoloured the paintings.

They deleted the murals.
They devastated the fields.
They decarbonated the soft drinks.
They decorticated the trees.
They deflowered the gardens.
They dispersed the herds.
They disyoked the oxen.
They devalued the currency.
They decelerated the cars.
They declutched the motors.
They decocted the soups.
They decompressed the airplanes.
They disappropriated industries.
They decertified the unions.
They disinherited the orphans.
They deported the citizens.
They depressed the prelates.
They deserted the sick.
They disparaged the old.
They dispatched the unwanted.
They disgraced themselves daily.
They despised the truth.
They disunited brothers.
They decerebrated the birds.
They dechlorinated the water.
They deluded the faithful.
They discredited the economy.
They derailed the trains.
They deranged the heads.
They disassembled the machines.

They dishallowed the sanctuaries.
They disheartened the women.
They disjointed the nation.
They dispossessed the poor.
They degerminated the seeds.
They dehumanized the men.
They delaminated the wood.
They deprived the workers.
They desiccated the wells.
They decimated the country.
They distorted the facts.
They discoursed daily.
They desalinated the sea.
They disrupted the flow.
They dissolved the achievements.
They destroyed the city.

31.

Spring revives nature.
The grasses are born.
The sick man feels revived.
The flowers are reborn in spring.
The flowers enamel the fields.
The resistance is reborn.
Triplets are born.
Blossoms are born on the branches.
The trunk bears branches.
Plants are born between the rocks.
The trees renew their leaves.
The beauty renews her wardrobe.
The tender leaves are curled up.
Chlorophyll colours the leaves.
The trees become peopled with leaves.
The flowers take on colour.
The daisies bloom.
Daisies have yellow hearts.
Trade blossoms in peacetime.
The city is still at war.

Caterpillars gnaw through the leaves.
Beggars gnaw on bones.
Rodents lack canines.
It is warm in spring.

A cloud of mist crowns the volcano.
A column of mist rises in the distance.
The trees crown themselves with flowers.
There are blossoms on the chestnut and
hazelnut trees.
The cherry trees have blossomed.
The fields turn green again.
The rye grows stalks already.
Rye is similar to wheat.

The wheat is turning green already.
Wheat is a grass.
The grains germinate.
The plants grow seeds.
The trees bear fruit.
The pomegranates bloom.
Pomegranate flowers are red.
The pods grow seeds.
The poppy has red flowers.
Poppies bloom among the wheat.
Amaryllis and amaranths bloom.
Onions bloom.
Onions make you weep.
The corn is breaking through already.
Dawn is breaking.
Birds hover.
The vines are in bud.
Helicopters hover over the city.

32.

The children swing.
The children climb trees.
The children eat green fruit.
Green fruit causes diarrhea.
The girls wear bows in their hair.
The girls skip over ropes.
Lambs and kids skip.
The snow melts in spring.
The rivers swell with the thaw.
Torrents flow down the mountain sides.
The torrent skips from rock to rock.
The water forms whirlpools over the rocks.

The migratory birds return.
The sap awakens in spring.
The hummingbird revives.
The season advances.
The poem advances.
Time advances.
The author is a man advanced in years.

33.

The grapes are ripening already.
The apples are already turning red.
Kites of many colours fly.
The dragonfly flies near the water.
The dragonfly has blue wings.
The animals rut.
The rams butt.
Pairs of butterflies whirl through the air.
The pigeon covers his mate.
The henchmen repress zealously.
The beauty causes jealousy.
The lizards sun themselves.
The lizards pursue each other.
The stallion mounts the mare.
The donkey mounts the mare.
The mare is the female of the stallion.
Grass carpets the earth.
Carpets cover the floor.
The cattle are out at pasture.
Toothpaste comes from a tube.
The cattle graze in the pasture.
The beasts cut the grass in the pasture
with their teeth.

34.

A patch covers the one-eyed man's eye.
The one-eyed man cannot see in one eye.
The one-eyed man's eye is opaque.
The moon is a satellite.
Satellites are opaque.
Moles see loam.

The sleeve covers the arm.
The sleeve is empty.
They covered him with bruises.
They maimed him. He lost his arm.
The hood covers the face.
They cover their crimes.

The radiologist covers himself with a lead apron.
Flesh covers the skeleton.
X-rays penetrate the flesh.
Skeletons have bones.
The skeletons of children are small.
On black film bones are grey.
The bones are small.
The bones are twisted.
The bones are soft.
The children are undernourished.
Malnutrition causes rickets.
The small body covers itself with flesh.

The tyrant covers his neck.
The tyrant covers his chest with his hand.
He makes promises. Believe me he begs.
Fart rhymes with heart.
Feathers cover the bodies of birds.
The hat covers the head.
The First Lady uses a hat with feathers.
The peacock's mate is grey.
His crimes were discovered.
He uncovered himself before a lady.
From high up you can discover the countryside.
A mountain dominates the city.
The old man is not a dominant figure.
The old man dominates his passions.
The dominant colour is grey.
You can see the whole city from here.
A cable car goes to the top.
At the top there is a Virgin.
The procession climbs up the mountain.
The officers climb up through the ranks.
The officers wear epaulets.
The sword is worn on the belt.
The sword makes blood.
The procession carries banners.
The procession sings psalms.
The procession goes inside.

They discover an arsenal.
They discover arms and ammunition.
They discover medical equipment.
A doctor is put on trial.
An officer discovers with disgust
a drop of blood in his egg.

35.

The lips cover the teeth.
The beauty has crimson lips.
The beauty has coral lips.
The beauty paints her lips.
The beauty advertises a lipstick.
The beauty uses lipstick by *Quivlon.*
The beauty smiles.
The beauty has teeth of pearl.
The beauty brushes her teeth.
The beauty advertises a toothpaste.
The beauty uses toothpaste by *Pearlodent.*

The loincloth covers the private parts.
The foreskin covers the glans.
A blush covers the face.
The beauty blushes.
The beauty is single.
The beauty is dressed as a bride.
The beauty blushes easily.
The beauty has red cheeks.
The beauty uses cream blush.
The beauty advertises a cream blush.
The beauty uses cream blush by *Shy-N-Sweet.*

Pantyhose covers the legs.
The beauty has long legs.
The beauty sways her hips.
The beauty shows off her legs.
The beauty advertises pantyhose.
The beauty uses pantyhose by *Silkolex*.

36.

The streets are covered with fliers.
The sky is covered with whitish clouds.
The beach is covered with conch shells.
The veil covers the face.
The priest covers the chalice.
Water plants cover the lagoon.
Algae cover the lagoon.
The gardener covers the plants with mulch.
Glass covers the greenhouse.
The pasture is covered with thistles.
Brambles cover the fences.
The shepherd rescues a kid from the brambles.
A boardwalk goes by the sea.
The beauty walks rhythmically.
The acrobat walks on a tightrope.
The old man walks slowly.
The cripple walks with a limp.
The sleepwalker walks in his dream.
The citizens walk with their heads down.
The bishop walks diagonally.
The invalid walks on crutches.
The blind man walks with a cane.

37.

The blind man is feeling his way.
The blind man has a very keen ear.
Sounds are perceived by the ear.
I hear whispering voices.
Whispering wind.
Whispering water.
I hear indistinct voices.
I hear undefinable sounds.
I hear steps.
I hear whistling.
I hear car horns.
I hear the bustle of the street.

The blind man is groping his way.
The blind man goes by touch.
The fear is tangible.

I heard bursts of machine gun fire.
The machine guns rattled.
I heard tanks roll.
I heard airplanes fly low.
Explosions reverberated.
The explosions shattered the silence.
Then silence.
Tarara! goes the trumpet.
The sound of the trumpet is piercing.
I hear military bands.

The fife is shrill.
Boom! goes the bass drum.
I hear soldiers march.
I hear snare drums.
The drums roll.
Rat-a-tat! go the drums.
I hear bugles play.
The bugles sound shrill.
I hear shouts of command.

I lost my eyesight as a child.
I have lost the memory of my face.
The blind man counts the steps.
I hear strange noises.
I hear sobbing voices.
I hear lamenting.
I hear the whistle of a train.
I hear weeping.
You can hear the surf roar.

I hear grumbling.
I hear swearwords.
I hear moans.
I hear boisterous laughter.
I hear absurd things.
I hear panting.
The ringing of cash registers.
Squealing brakes.
A drill pierces the pavement.
The bells ring clearly.

Loose horseshoes clatter.
The wagon wheels screech.
The peasants go to market.
The merchants praise their wares.
The buyers bargain.
The street vendors hawk their goods.
I smell rubber wine fruit pears apples.
I smell anise cumin cloves.
I smell fragrant flowers.
I smell musk garlic.
I smell rancid repugnant nauseating smells.

I hear the cry of the newborn.
I hear the scream of the virgin.
I hear the gasp of the dying.

The city is an immense cave never
    reached by daylight.
The city is the murmuring darkness of a great
    subterranean river.
The city smells deafens hushes stinks.
The city is the tomb of the sea.
The shell to which I press my ear.
A beehive invaded by ants.
The swarms disperse and the queens nest
    in my ears.

The blind man has a very keen nose.
The fishermen smell of fish.
The firemen smell of smoke.
The carpenters smell of wood.
The newspaper boys of ink.
The sick of medicine.
The gravediggers of grave.
The shoemakers of leather.
The greedy of money.
The tyrant's agents smell of rat.
The agents try to coax me.
They threaten me.
They even offer me money.
To them I am blind and mute.
Leave this poor blind man in peace.
Let me play my guitar in peace.

38.

For now I do not know who you are
nor where you are always.
I know it was our lot to live
in the same city
and in the same country on the earth
at the same time.
And that is enough.

Today it is night, but tomorrow
I shall go out like yesterday in search of you.
I am sure to recognize you.
Just in case, so that you know,
I shall walk as always
with black glasses and a white cane.

39.

There is an invasion of rats.
The rats overrun the granaries.
The rats invade the houses.
They nest in the garrets.
They attack the animals in packs.
They bite a newborn child.
The rats screech at night.
There are not enough rat traps.
The cats get ill from eating too many rats.
The poisoned rats stink.
The rats have mange.
Mange is contagious.
The rats spread the plague.
The rats infest the city.
The city is in quarantine.
They watch the ships.
The ships are in quarantine.
They spray the buildings.
They exterminate and vaccinate.
They disinfect the city.
The vaccine immunizes.
The city stinks.
The city is unhealthy.
The city is isolated.
Patients with contagious diseases are isolated.
The plague speads very fast.

The plague is a devastating epidemic.
An epidemic reigns.
The water is contaminated.
The atmosphere is polluted.
The atmosphere is unbreathable.
The language is contaminated.

40.

The dogs hunt mice.
The dog watches the house.
The dog watches the flock.
The dog is easy to train.
They train dogs for torture.
The dog has a black muzzle.
They remove the muzzle.
The dog bites.
They goad the dog on.

Dogs have keen hearing.
The dog pricks up his ears.
The dog growls.
The dog flashes his teeth.
The dogs bark.
They call the dog.

The dog licks his plate.
The waves lick the coast.
The dog gnaws on a bone.
The bone has marrow.

They punish the dog.
The dog disobeys.
The dog whines.
The politicians lick their lips.
The dog licks the hand that punishes him.

41.

The beauty washes her hair.
The breeze caresses her caramel-coloured hair.
The breeze caresses her corkscrew-curled hair.
The beauty advertises a shampoo.
The beauty washes her hair with shampoo
    by *Curlicue*.
The beauty is blonde.
The beauty colours her hair.
The shoeshine boys colour leather.
The beauty uses hair colouring by *Quairol.*
The beauty combs her hair.
The old man combs his hair.
His hair is white.
The old man is white-haired.
The old man is white-bearded.
The tyrant is aging.
The tyrant is getting fat.
The tyrant uses a girdle.
The tyrant uses hair colouring by *Quairol.*
The beauty has silky hair.
Silk is soft.
The beauty seduces.
The beauty fascinates.
The serpent fascinates the birds.
The beauty is a model.

The beauty is to be imitated.
Tinsel imitates gold.
The models show dresses.
The models parade.
Independence is celebrated once a year
The troops parade before the tyrant.
The streets are decorated.
Medals decorate the tyrant's uniform.
They hang up streamers.
The sword hangs from the belt.
The sword is made of white metal.
The beauty is white.
The beauty powders her face.
The beauty applies cosmetics.
Cosmetics beautify the skin.
The beauty has lily-white skin.
They cover up their crimes.
Cosmetics cover up blemishes.
The beauty has a long neck.
Swans are white.
The beauty has a swan neck.
Geese have webbed feet.
The cadets parade in goose-step.
The cadets are gallant.
They are in gala uniforms.
The infantry parades in squares.
The troops parade in columns.
The soldiers wear backpacks.
The bishops wear mitres.
Guns are worn over the shoulder.

The barrel leans on the shoulder.
They fire a salute.
The old man leans on a cane.
The beauty leans towards the Junta.
The beauty is chosen Miss Metropolis.
The beauty is chosen Miss Universe.
The beauty poses for the photographers.
The beauty sighs.
The sigh denotes some feeling.
The beauty appears on covers.
The beauty advertises.
The beauty sells.
The beauty is the most beautiful woman
in the world.
The beauty and the tyrant embrace.
The beauty hangs on the tyrant's neck.
The beauty is the goddess of the city.
The beauty is a false goddess.

42.

The river cuts the city in two.
The river separates the city.
Beyond the river live the poor.
Here the rich.
Reeds grow along the riverbanks.
My cradle had a curtain of gauze.
Gauze absorbs blood.
Reeds are woven into baskets and blinds.
The heron lives on the riverbank.
Willows grow on riverbanks.
The roots burrow into the earth.
The roots absorb.
The river carries silt.
Silt absorbs water.
They dredge the harbour entrance.
The river bathes the walls of the city.
Weeds grow on the walls.
The artillery batters the walls.
The waves batter the cliffs.
The cook mixes the batter.
He does not bat an eye.
The sun bathes the room.
The washerwomen bathe in the river.
The gypsies bathe pots in zinc.
The confectioner bathes fruit in syrup.
The soldiers are bathed in blood.

The mourners are bathed in tears.
The widows wear black.
Black absorbs light rays.
Certain waters turn objects into stone.
On this side, sparrows in sight.
On that side, swallows alight.

43.

Water is the element of fish.
Fish cannot live out of water.
The fishermen dream of fish.
The fish dream of worms.
The branches of the willows hang to the ground.
The fishing line hangs from the rod.
The fishing line disappears in the water.
The mosquitoes sting.
The fish refuse to bite.
The fish jump up from the water.
The fish dive.
The submarines dive.
They went underground.
Fish are slippery.
Fish have bones.
The agents make no bones.
They throw the net from land.
Fish fall into the net.
Live fish are kept in the fishbowl.
They stick their tongues out at them.
Fish cannot live out of water.
The fishbowl contains water.
Fish are covered with scales.
The prisoners are covered with bruises.
The seagull feeds on fish.
The seal feeds on fish.
The whale feeds on plankton.
The whale tears the fishermen's nets.

There are caterpillars in the garden.
The blind man suffered from cataracts.
They cater to the wealthy.
New cadres have been trained.
In the resistance they will harden.
The struggle takes on more refined forms.
The needle is fine.
The thread goes through the needle's eye.
The shoemaker sews with waxed thread.
The seamstress hems.
The old man hems.

44.

The professor passes out tests.
They take the professor from the classroom.
They take stones from the quarry.
The tongue passes over the lips.
In the shopwindows are delicacies.
The hungry lick their lips.
The mouth organ passes before the lips.
The unemployed repair the streets.
Food repairs.
I do not earn the food for the day.
I cheat my hunger.
The charlatan cheats the gullible.
The charlatan takes out money.
They pass counterfeit bills.
One automobile passes another.
They passed him a report.
We pass penury.
We pass furriers.
The hours pass.
The cuckoo leaves the wooden clock.
The cuckoo strikes the hour.
Cuckoo! goes the cuckoo.
The mailman passes from house to house.
They weigh the letters.
They weigh the newborn.
The boxers weigh themselves.
Remorse weighs heavily.
The boxers hit each other.

The player hits the ball.
The player makes a pass.
The quarterback passes the ball to the goalie.
The clapper hits the bell.
The blows make him queasy.
The drumstick hits the drum.
The gong is hit with a mallet.
Electric shocks vibrate.
Electric shocks contort.
The tortured writhe.
The shocks leave crimson marks.
Crimson is the colour of cardinals.
The cardinal prays for the missing.

48.

The river flows against the current.
The water runs up the waterfall.
The people start walking backwards.
The horses walk backwards.
The soldiers unmarch the parade.
The bullets leave the flesh.
The bullets enter the barrels.
The officers put their pistols away.
Electricity returns through the cords.
Electricity passes through the plugs.
The tortured stop shaking.
The tortured close their mouths.
The concentration camps empty.
The missing appear.
The dead rise from their graves.
The jets fly backwards.
The bombs rise towards the jets.
Allende fires.
The flames die down.
He takes off his helmet.
La Moneda rebuilds itself entirely.
His skull repairs itself.
He steps out on a balcony.
Allende backs up towards Tomás Moro.
The prisoners leave the stadium backwards.
September 11.
Airplanes full of refugees return.
Chile is a democratic country.

The armed forces respect the constitution.
The military go back to their barracks.
Neruda is reborn.
He returns by ambulance to Isla Negra.
His prostate hurts. He writes.
Victor Jara plays the guitar. He sings.
The speeches enter the mouths.
The tyrant embraces Prats.
He disappears. Prats revives.
The unemployed are rehired.
The workers parade singing.
We shall overcome!

49.

The path is the continuation of the road.
The road leads to the city.
Summer is the continuation of spring.
The curfew continues.
The misery continues.
The repression continues.
It is hot.
The heat continues.
The poem continues.
The schoolchildren leave on vacation.
The soldiers leave for the battlefield.
Highways leave the city.
The troops make camp.
The animals sleep in the open.
The soldiers in tents.
The wheat fields were turning green.
The troops ran across the fields.
The passage of the troops destroyed the crops.
The granaries are empty.
They mow the fields.
The sickle is curved.
The scythe is curved.
The scythe mows at ground level.
The snake hisses.

The child carries water to the mowers.
The grain passes through the screen.
The hulls are stripped from the grain.
The grain is separated from the straw.
Wheat contains much straw.
The straw is gathered with a pitchfork.
The straw is stored in the barn.
The grain falls between the millstones.
Wheat is made into flour.
Flour is made into bread.
Bread nourishes.
The bread gets stale.
They feed stale bread to the beggars.

50.

The city is steaming.
The city is an oven.
The baker is kneading the bread.
The dough is made with water and flour.
The rolling-pin flattens the dough.
The bread bakes in the oven.
The baker's oven is steaming.
Sweat comes out of the pores.
The baker is sweating.
The coals are steaming.
The dish on the table is steaming.

52.

The heat is stifling.
The hot air is stifling.
The faces turn red.
The heat dilates bodies.
The heat evaporates liquids.
The water level drops in the summer.
The reeds dry out.
The reeds are tangled.
The tangles are hard to pry loose.
A wave of arrests has been let loose.
There are regattas in the river.
They water the soil to refresh it.
Tanker trucks water the trees.
The trees provide shade.
The terrace has a canopy.
Canopies provide shade.
There are tables on the terrace.
Refreshments alleviate the heat.
The sun scorches the flowers.
Sprinklers water the flowers.
The sun is an efficient source of heat.

53.

Intense heat awaits us.
I am waiting to win the lottery.
I am waiting for a friend in the shade.
The trees offer sweet shade.
The trees produce fruit.
The fruit comes after the blossoms.
The fruit contains the seed.
They are reaping the fruit of the dictatorship.
The roses have long stems.
The glasses have long stems.
They drink champagne.
They are drinking a toast to the tyrant.
The sun ripens the fruit.
The fruit takes on colour.
They paint the fruit.
The painter paints some fruit.
His thumb is in the palette.
The brush applies the colour.
The paint is fresh.
The paint is drying.
The fruit is in season.
The birds peck at the fruit.
The birds sit in the trees.
The tyrant is sitting for a portrait.
The branches sag under the weight of the fruit.
The fruit tears as it ripens.
Fallen fruit rots.

The tyrant will fall and rot.
The pig has a big head.
The cap covers the head.
The pig has drooping ears.
Glasses sit on the ears.
The pig uses dark glasses.
The glasses sit on the nose.
The pig's face is nearly square.
The pig roots among the fallen fruit.
The pig grunts.
The pig feeds a tapeworm.
The tapeworm is several meters long.
The anaconda is several meters long.

54.

The earth turns around the sun.
The merry-go-round has wooden horses.
The merry-go-round turns.
The potter's wheel turns.
The roulette wheel turns.
The revolver drum turns.
The tank turret turns.
There is a weather vane on the tower.
The weather vane turns.
The top turns.
The windmills turn.
The propellers turn.
The dancers turn.
Sunflowers turn yellow.
Gold is yellow.
The soldiers file out.
One follows the other.
The computer is filled with files.
The file is made of tempered steel.
The file has teeth.
The bars are made of iron.
The file bites into the iron.
The lemons are turning yellow.
The cornfields are turning yellow.
Corn has yellow grains.
Gold is yellow.
Gold is brilliant.
The stars are brilliant.

Jell-O is yellow.
The surf forms billows.
The cans scintillate.
Topaz is yellow.
The windowpanes glitter.
The sun is hard on the eyes.
The egg yolk is yellow.
The yolk coagulates.
The butter melts.
The canary eats grains.
The canary is yellow.
The grain is stored in the silo.
The silos are empty.
The canary has no grain in its feeder.

55.

They adhered to the agreement.
They dug diligently on their knees.
They opened a breach in the wall.
They finished the hole.
Free rhymes with flee.
They fled under cover of night.
The fugitives acted in concert with others.
They are beating someone.
The prisoners are beating on the bars.
The darkness favoured their flight.
They pursued them with bloodhounds.
They fled along the sewers.
They fled over rugged terrain.
They accused a guard of complicity.
The police pursue the fugitives.
Modern rifles range far.
They reached one of the fugitives.
An ambulance picked up the wounded one.
The poor receive alms.
The shepherds collect the cattle.
They ran over undulating terrain.
The jeep travels over uneven terrain.
They ran across flooded orchards.
Oleander has purple flowers.
They entered flowering oleander fields.
Helicopters fly like bees.
Helicopters drone like bees.

Bees hum.
Ears hum.
The fugitives are panting.
The bees sting.
The puma seizes a lamb.
The lamb bleats.
Anyone who harbours fugitives will be punished.
Priests protect the fugitives.

56.

The heat dries up the torrents.
The sea water evaporates.
The salt water lagoons dry out.
Salt remains in the dried marshes.
Salt solidifies in the salt mines.
Salty soil is sterile.
Clay bricks dry in the sun.
Tobacco leaves are drying.
Underwear is drying in the patio.
They are hanging up laundry.
The beggars hold out their hands.
The sun dries the laundry.
The plants are getting dry.
The sick man's skin is dry.
He is losing his hair.
His face is inflamed.
The sick man is a monster.
Sores cover his body.
The alligator is covered with scales.
Scales are forming on the sick man's skin.
Scales overlap.
Shingles overlap.
The patient gasps.

Fish gasp.
Fish is fried in boiling oil.
The boiling oil splutters.
The wood sends out sparks.
Smoke comes from the roof.
The fire crackles.
The burning wood crackles.
The patient is ablaze with fever.
The house is ablaze.

57.

Air makes combustion possible.
Air is indispensable for life.
Air makes respiration possible.
Air is the carrier of sound.
The arrow rends the air.
We don't have enough air.
The dictatorship stifles.
The dictatorship strangles.
They strangled him with a wire.
He died by strangulation.

The tyrant is choking.
The tyrant has trouble swallowing.
They pat him on the back.
He brings up a mouthful.
He stains his gala uniform.
He spatters over his decorations.
The ladies tuck up their finery.
They wrinkle their noses.
They fan him.
The fan makes air.
Air! Air!

The tyrant has us choking.
We have the tyrant stuck in our throats
like a fishbone.
We have the tyrant stuck like a splinter
between flesh and fingernail.
We have the tyrant stuck like a piece of
dirt in the eye.
The piece of dirt makes millions shed tears.
We have the tyrant stuck in the rectum.
The tyrant is a hard, intractable piece of shit.

58.

The sea air tans the face.
The sun burns.
They burn incense in the church.
Candles burn in the church.
The fire melts the candles.
The beauty is sunbathing.
The beauty is toasting.
The beauty uses a bathing suit.
The beauty has smooth flesh.
Flesh spoils in the heat.
Flesh decomposes rapidly in summer.
Decomposition is a sure sign of death.

59.

Christmas is approaching.
New Year's Eve is approaching.
My end is approaching.
The end of the poem is approaching.
December is the twelfth month of the year.
December has 31 days.
The old man tells about his childhood.
They tear the last sheet off the calendar.
The old man leaves the womb.
Happy New Year!
Rockets rise.
They burst in the night.
A rain of colours falls.
Firecrackers explode.
The old man sees the light.
The sun illuminates the earth.
The sun emits rays.
Crystal is transparent.
Light passes through crystal.
There is dust in the sunbeam.
The acetylene light glares.
The glare of the sun is incomparable.
The old man is in diapers.
The old man open his toothless mouth.
Milk comes from the mammary glands.
The milk is warm.
The milk is white and sweet.

The old man is nursing.
They bind the old man's navel.
His mouth is drooling.
The old man uses a bib.
The mother is tender.
The mother rocks the cradle.
The old man shakes the rattle.
The old man urinates all over himself.
The urine is warm.
The old man cries.
They are changing the old man.
The old man crawls.
The old man babbles.
The old man toddles.
The old man walks.
The old man starts to talk.
Things have names.
Persons have names.
The godfather scatters coins.
They christen the old man.
More! shout the children.
The old man names.
The old man names himself.
The shadow follows.
The old man is surprised.
The shadow imitates.
The shadow is mute.
The echo repeats.
The silence responds.
The old man paints childish figures.

The old man draws monkey faces.
Monkeys look like people.
The old man apes.
The old man is naive.
The old man plays.
The old man plays all the time.
He invents a toy city.

60.

The old man regards himself in the mirror.
The mirror repeats images.
The poem is a mirror.
Twins are identical.
They dressed us alike.
I am opposed to the government.
My brother is on the opposite side.
The brothers do not get along.
One says white.
The other says black.
On says red.
The other says black.

Ink is black.
Paper is white.
The old man writes by hand.
He wrinkles a piece of paper.
The old man has wrinkled skin.
The shortsighted use glasses.
The old man uses glasses.
The old man is in poor health.
The old man revises.
The eraser erases what was written.
Instead of a building it leaves a vacant lot.
A change in syntax reverses the flow of the river.
A period detains the city.
The earth is immobile in space.

The sea is immobile.
Time does not pass.
Nothing moves.
The inhabitants are paralyzed.
Immobility reigns.
An invisible snow falls.
Only the old man's fingers move.
The old man re-reads.
The old man's fingers run over the letters.
The old man finds the tyrant's name.
The old man erases his name.
His name does not deserve to be remembered.
The old man finds the assassins' names.
The old man erases the assassins' names.
Their names will not be forgotten.
Their hour of punishment will come.

61.

Cardboard laurels crown the old man.
It is the old man's birthday.
The cake is covered with icing.
The cake has candles.
The old man blows.
One candle is still burning.
The old man blows out the last candle.
They sing in the darkness.
The sound fades away.
Sound fades as the distance increases.
Happy Birthday!
Rockets rise.
They burst in the night.
A rain of colours falls.
Firecrackers explode.

62.

The people embrace.
We embraced when he left the stadium.
The son embraced his father.
The father embraced his daughter.
The daughter embraced her mother.
The mother embraced her son.
The brothers embraced.
Husband and wife embraced.
Rifles have brazen parts.

63.

The heat is like a brazier.
The fire is setting the forests ablaze.
The forest fed the fire.
The branches were ablaze.
The tree trunks were ablaze.
The heat is devastating.
The heat devastates the fields.
The heat razes the crop.
The desert is arid.
The earth is turning arid.
The soil is cracking.
The cracks meander.
The wind stirs up whirlpools of dust.
The dry bed of the creek meanders.
The wind drags along dust clouds.
The earth is parched.
The drought harms the harvest.
The earth asks for water.
The vehicles stir up dust clouds.

Varnish protects from dust.
The carpenter varnishes a piece of furniture.
Dust gathers under the furniture.
Swish! Swish! goes the broom.
They tar the streets.
The tar keeps the dust down.
The wound becomes inflamed from the dust.

64.

The wound is bleeding.
The wound breaks open every day.
It breaks open at sunrise.
Night falls.
The wound does not close.
The days pass.
The years pass.
The wound does not close.
The wound bleeds secretly.
The wound is stanched behind walls.
The wound bleeds in cells.
The wound bleeds behind barbed wire.
The wound is a mouth.
A bandage gags it.
The wound is a toothless old mouth.
The wound mutters with naked gums.
The wound hurts.
They put it to sleep.
He wakes up hurting every day.
The wound hurts at night.
At night the soldiers hear it in the empty streets.
They hear it behind closed windows and doors.
It is like the sound of painful kisses.
It is woes and moans.
It is the lips of the wound which close and open.
It is the wounded moaning in their dreams.

The wound does not let you sleep.
The wound does not let you live.
At night the tyrant's minions pick at the wound.
They irritate it deepen it.
They silence it with music at full volume.
The wound forms pus.
The wound suppurates.
The light cleans the wound every day.
At night it becomes infected.
No one escapes from the wound.
They whole city is wounded.
Many are wounded without knowing it.
They think they are safe and sound.
They are wounded.
The wound is just a nuisance. They forget it.
They think they are invulnerable.
They are wounded.
They celebrate victory. They are wounded.
They enjoy power. They are wounded.
They sing. They dance. They get fat.
They are wounded.
The victorious are fatally wounded.

Many others pretend there is no wound.
They hide it. They deny it.
The wound makes them feel ashamed.
They medicate the wound.
They anoint it.
They cover it with gauze. They stop it with cotton.
They change the bandages every day.

The wound does not heal.
They treat it with home remedies.
They cover it with compresses of mud
        and spiderwebs.
They pray.
The wound does not heal.
The wound oozes.
Blood soaks the bandages.
The wound betrays them.
The wound denounces the hypocrites.
They were accomplices.
Some of them still are.
The gravely wounded survive in pain.
The remainder should be dead.
So terrible so vast is the wound.
Nobody can explain how they survive.
They are a wound.
The wound is all they have.
All that is left. All they are allowed to have.
The wound denounces.
They prohibit showing the wound.
The wound identifies us.
By the wound they recognize each other.
The wound unites them.
The wound is a password.
They clench their teeth.
They clench their fists.
The wound is a ragged flag.

The tyrant's green wound stinks.
His wound has died.
His wound has rotted away.
The tyrant is a living corpse.
The tyrant befouls the air he breathes.
He lives in isolation.
Far from his wife.
Far from his family.
His bodyguards avoid his breath.
Pestilence surrounds the tyrant.

They probe the wound.
They ask when until when how far.
The wound is unfathomable.
The wound will heal with time.
The tyrant will rot and fall.
Those who wound will be punished.
The fatally wounded will die.
The wound will leave a scar.
The scar will not be wiped out.
The wound will not be forgotten.
The scar will mark us forever.

65.

Dead calm.
One can hear the cicadas.
The foliage rustles.
The frogs croak.
One can hear the crickets.
Hush! Hush! they ask for quiet.
Shush! Shush! they impose silence.
The dogs howl.
The crickets are quiet.
The cricket hides in a hole.
The violins of the orchestra are quiet.
The sea is quiet.
One hears rumbling.
The rumbling grows.
The rumbling comes closer.
Quake! Earthquake!
The lamps swing.
The windows rattle.
The floor boards creak.
A fine dust falls from the ceiling.
The people protect themselves under the lintels.
One can hear screams.
Tables and chairs shake.
The lights go off and on.
The pictures slide on the walls.
The dishes fall.

The city shudders.
Plates break.
Glasses break.
Pieces of cornice fall.
The earth moves.
Cracks open in the ground.
Cracks form in the walls.
Earthquake!
The houses the buildings totter.
The earthquake stuns.
The houses shake.
The walls rock back and forth.
The walls tremble.
The floor trembles.
The windowpanes splinter.
The earth shakes itself.
The city shakes itself.
The city splits up.
Panic reigns.
The ground rocks.
The buildings sway.
The cables tighten.
The cables are cut.
The posts topple over.
Shingles fall.
The faithful cross themselves.
The ambulances wail.
One hears the sirens of fire engines.
The ambulances run an obstacle course.
The quake is over.
One hears screams shouts.

The children cry with fear.
The city remains standing.
The curfew remains.
The state of siege remains.
The state of civil war remains.
The panic passes.
The city calms down.
They bury the victims.
They clear the streets.
They collect assistance for the homeless.
They rebuild the city.
The old man reconstructs the facts.

66.

Were the streets wet?

No. They were dry.

Was it cold?

No. It was warm.

Was it winter?

No. It was summer.

What time was it?

Late.

Was the house dark?

No. The lights were on.

What colour was the automobile?

Grey.

How many automobiles were there?

Two.

What colour was the other automobile?

Grey.

Were there people in the street?

No.

Had the curfew begun yet?

Yes.

Were there patrols in the streets?

Yes.

The city was silent.

The streets were empty.

Were the children awake?

The children were asleep.
The children play all day.
The children were tired.
The children were asleep.

Did you hear the automobiles arrive?

No.

What were you doing when the automobiles arrived?

There were dirty dishes in the sink.
I was washing the dishes.
The man was tired.
The man was sitting in the armchair.
The armchair is comfortable.
Several men entered the house.
Basketball players are tall.
Bodyguards are muscular.
A woman opened the door.
She is slim.
Our house is the first one on the block.
It is white.
The bakery is around the corner.
The man got up from the armchair.

How were the men dressed?

Normally.

Were the men in uniforms?

No. They were in plain clothes.

What were the men like?

Basketball players are tall.
Bodyguards are muscular.

67.

They beheaded us.
They felled the tree.
They quartered us.
They cut the trunk into logs.
They cut off the branches.
The roots lived on.
The roots stayed in the ground.
The roots grow under the ground.
New shoots are growing from the stump.

The heart beats.
The arteries beat.
The resistance has gone underground.
The feet support.
The dispersed regroup.
The leg comes between the hip and the foot.
The feet walk.
The resistance regroups.
The fibula is joined to the tibia.
The parties reorganize.
New strength is gathered.
The knee is the joint between thigh and leg.
The strength is refocussed.
The thigh goes from the hip to the knee.
The resistance is united.

In the groin the thigh unites with the belly.
The parties unite.
At the hip the thigh joins the trunk.
The parties join efforts.
Their interests coincide.
The chest goes from the belly to the neck.
The parties form a whole.
The neck joins the head to the trunk.
The head contains the brain.
The resistance is one.
The head is one.
The head is raised high.
The parties act in unison.
The line of vertebrae forms the spine.
We persist in our resolve.
The thorax contains the heart and the lungs.
The lungs regenerate the blood.
The resistance persists.
The blood nourishes the muscles.
The workers sabotage.
The resistance rallies.
The workers start a slowdown.
The workers fold their arms.
Civil servants refuse to do lunch.
The muscles palpitate.
The miners refuse to enter the cafeterias.
They banish the leaders.
The heart palpitates.
The workers go on strike.

As long as the heart palpitates there is life.
The dictatorship is reversible.
The dictatorship will not last.
We reaffirm our will to fight.
The heart is the size of a fist.

68.

The athlete reaches the finish line.
The mountain climber reaches the summit.
At the end of the railway line there is a buffer.
The bus reaches the terminal.
The poem reaches its end.
The old man finishes the poem.
His life is ending.
The old man makes his will.
The poem is his last will and testament.
One cannot devine the future.
The year 2000 is a leap year.
February has 28 days in normal years.
February has 29 days in leap years.
The year 1996 is a leap year.
The year 1992 is a leap year.
The year 1988 was a leap year.
The year 1984 was a leap year.
The year 1980 was a leap year.

The old man is still breathing.
The old man is approaching the end.
These are his final verses:

And after going with closed eyes
through the darkness that guides us
to open one's eyes and see the darkness
        that guides us
with open eyes and to close one's eyes.

The poem closes.

III.

A Strange House

1. Vae Victis!

Scaffolds, 1979
Tape and Plastic Film

Indignation tends to compose verses.

Miguel de Cervantes

Ideas

My mink fur is beautiful.
They hunt me for it.
They catch me. For it
they kill me. They skin me.

The Capture

You did not imagine that the noise
of an automobile in the night
violating the curfew
with impunity
and turning in to your street
heading towards your house
and finally stopping outside
could silence the city
make the silence roar.

Interrogation

Stuck to the mouth
dry with fear
the tongue
wants saliva.

The silence
and the word
kill.

From the gullet
suddenly gushes
the cry,
          for water.

Firing squad

For Raúl Barrientos

Kneeling
        against the wall
under the blanket
        he awaits his hour
while behind his back
        laughing
soldiers point
        at the eyes in the soles
of his final shoes.

Stadium

To flee from torture,
trapeze artist without net,
acrobat without tightrope,
you hurled yourself into the void.
But you were not high enough:
you survived the somersault.
You will die begging for death,
tortured till the end
on the track.

The Transfer

We whisper for the last time
on the refrigerated truck
like clams barely open
on a tin plate.
Later with our mouths shut
we shall bite the cold knife.

Turkish Bath

If the blindfold were to slip
you would confirm that the place
where you find yourself naked
and blind is a deserted
and stifling Turkish bath.
You hear water run in showers,
and on naked flesh,
resonant among moans,
the slaps of masseurs.

The Break

They go off like flies
walking around on the ceiling
and turn the volume down
to listen to music
and not my screams for a while.

They peel fruit and smoke,
joking among themselves
and with me, while I hang
upside down by my feet.

Concentration Camp in Spring

Is is somewhat encouraging to discover
that the fence posts
take root and sprout buds again,
barbed wire in the flesh
and wounds oozing resin.

Jail

He told me: some
people grow
beween bars
and reach the street
from the sewer
like ferns.

Vigilance

Although at all times
we are spied on maliciously
one rarely catches
a toothless child
smiling cruelly
when discovered
among the treetops.

While

While they come to get her
around dawn, in plain clothes,
four armed men.
While they search her desk.
While they ask her
to accompany them for a little chat.
While she is taken to heaquarters.
While she enters the secret building.
While she listens, among screams
of others under torture.
While she refuses
to sign a confession,
but must do so under duress.
While they force her to drink
a cup of tea containing
an undissolved capsule.
While they advise her to cooperate.
While they warn her that
she'd better obey.
While they make her undress
and hand her a blanket.
While the doctor asks her
about past and present ailments.
While they mark both nipples
with iodine crosses.
While they paint her ankles, her lower abdomen,
with iodine.

While they apply electrodes
to the painted areas.
While they turn on the current.
While she convulses among the wires.
While she screams.
While she jumps on the grill,
entangling herself in the wires.
While they raise the voltage
and she screams herself hoarse.
While they destroy her innards.
While she grinds her teeth.
While she gives off sparks.
While they make her wet.
While she passes out
and is returned to her dungeon.
You startle and stir.
A vague nightmare wakes you up.
You have a drink of water.
You go back to sleep.
You sleep peacefully.

The Henchman Also Goes on Vacation

By day he swims in the ocean
that holds some of his victims.
By night he hears the booming
blows of the waves
against wet towels.
Up at sunrise he fears but examines
what the tide hurls
against the beach at night:
these shattered jellyfish, these twisted
squid with almost human eyes.

2. 49th Parallel

The climate of Canada is everywhere of that invigorating quality which urges man to his greatest efforts.

A World Geography for Canadian Schools
(Toronto: Denton and Lord, 1936)

Atlases

They say that one could
people a continent
with the exiles of the century.
But there are no Americas left.
Perhaps Atlantis.

The Umbrella Doctor

We are leaving. And even
the umbrella doctor
abandons his shop and emigrates
to climates he considers more propitious
– he does not know that acid rains, radioactive
cyclones await him – he points out:
impossible to mend the holes
from this downpour of bullets.

The Last Supper

For Silverio Muñoz

My diviner friend buries his hand
in the entrails
          and holds up
the obsidian-green liver of the bird.

We carefully scrutinize its folds.
An enigma is the gem of crystallized bile
to the people,
          and it augurs long years
in power for the tyrant.
We shall leave for exile in a few days.
Who knows if we shall see each other again.

We shall go our own ways.
Let us toast now, what else can we do,
and eat rice and saffron with
this tasty sacred chicken.

Exit

To the passengers whose password was:
"Piscina aperta, tempo permettendo".

We left Chile on board the Rossini
and sailed for as long as the author
took to compose *The Barber of Seville*:
thirteen or fourteen days.

As we crossed the Panama Canal
we saw a shoe
floating in the Miraflores lock.

I did not ask myself
where we would go, once on land,
when the Panamanian visa
expired in a week.

My only obsession was to learn
whether it was a right or a left shoe,
on what foot it had belonged.

Stateless

The plane that just landed
deposited me on an airmail envelope
the size of an airport.
I carry neither address nor sender.
I have no names or luggage.

The loudspeakers
announce my arrival amplifying
the supersonic whistling of space
and metal detector birds
signal my transit
with strident trills.

In future my barrier
will be the horizon, serrated edge
forever.
          I stick to the wall
with my back, gummy with sweat;
after the flash a stamp canceller,
red hot to brand me,
searches for my face.

Portable Typewriter

Then he writes postcards
on a typewriter carved
out of toilet soap
with taciturn fingers:
"There are beautiful butterflies
in Costa Rica,
and in Canada much snow,
vast forests, and lakes.

Byward Market. Ottawa

Look at me,
the pride of the family orchard,
now an export product.
Listen to my unrecognizable name
and to my brain being hawked like cabbage
in this foreign labour market.
Pure and dirty, recently uprooted,
a white radish.

Winter

The days are short.
Long the nights. White
the immense common expanses.
When I go out I walk about hooded
like a monk in the corridors
of this monastery of the cold.
An X-ray sun
penetrates the forests
of naked branches and my skeleton
hands, ungloved.

Correspondence

From the South painfully far away
they come bundled and still
to break this chilling
and glittering routine.
On a truck they arrive
and are unloaded dead
friends in mailbags.

Hockey

Canadian death
glides towards me,
swiftly over the ice
like a hockey-player
wielding
his wooden scythe.
I don't even know how to skate,
I play soccer, I tell him.

Summer Tires

I have been here ten years,
he says, almost resigned,
like a summer tire
spinning on the spot,
skidding on the ice.

Mopping

To the cleaners
of 120 Holland Avenue, Ottawa

He applied for other jobs,
but he spoke neither English nor French.
And he will never speak them.
But he did learn
to count the years spent
mopping floors, washing dishes,
cleaning bathrooms:
"fibe, sic, seben, ei, nain,
ten, eleben ..."
And a new winter comes.
Once again, the snow and the tyrant will fall.

Tavern

The blue frigate of Molson beer
circumnavigates once more
its bottle, round like the world,
although it looks as if it had never moved,
like me and these old
hard-boiled pickled eggs,
from these shrines of solitude,
the saddest taverns on the planet.

Blue Jay

It flies past like a blue example
from the village to its nest in the forest,
before my window, this brilliant
challenge of cold monotony;
daily, this fleeting joy.

And what is this “blue jay” called,
the way I speak? *Arrendajo:*

A mocking bird with a jarring sound
that mimics the call of other birds:
“Good Morning”. “How are you”.
It learns to sing in captivity
some short and simple melodies.

Movie Theatre. Double Bill.

Movie actors feel as if they were living in exile.
Exiled not only from the stage, but also from themselves.

Luigi Pirandello

1. Dubbing

A character in a dubbed film
being shown in other countries
where his daily habits
are exotic,
and his movements and gestures
incomprehensible, slightly ridiculous.
As he opens his mouth to speak
of his beloved origin,
another voice in a strange language
supplants his silent tongue
and says: "Save your breath, brother!"

2. Pasolini's Salo or the 120 Days of Sodom

There are spectators who ask for asylum
almost as soon as they enter, in the Antechamber
of Hell. They are a minority.
The exodus becomes massive
in the Circle of Blood.
And the diaspora spreads even further
when in the Circle of Shit
a girl is force-fed
excrement with a teaspoon.
Many spectators
are leaving all the time
and coming back in.
The great majority, however,
their eyes closed or open,
stick it out until the end.

Greetings

My dear armadillo,
my condor and guanaco.
Greetings to you
from the moose and the elk,
the polar bear
and the flying squirrel.

Cassette

We speak in fractured voices,
tell jokes, sing in chorus,
toast among peals of laughter.
We record the crying of a baby,
the barking of a dog,
sobs, hacking cough
– not knowing that the tape
was jammed in the reel –
for distant listeners
who will hear only the echo of silence
when it reaches them.

Calendar

The geese fly South
as in a calendar picture
forming a V
that crumbles and restores itself:
the initial of the victim
or a remote victory.

You'd better not look up,
bury your eyes and your feet
in the first snow.
You spend another winter
with pigeons, starlings and sparrows.

Saint John River, N.B.

Today I make peace
with this generous land
thanks to this broad torrent,
this artery of the redskin buffalo
or the jugular of the Mapuche horse.
I who yesterday spit on its ice,
today reverently kiss
its sacred kindred waters.

3. A Strange House

Guardians of Appearances, 1980
Plastic Film

And had everything necessary to the Modern Man,
A phonograph, a radio, a car and a frigidaire.

W. H. Auden

The Object

Triumphantly I say to the object
I desire: Now you are mine.
The impenetrable object objects
opaquely: You buy me,
but you have not paid for my secret.

Bait

The fish's eyes
were always on us,
open and voracious, disproportionate like suns.

And we ignored them
with our blindness
of worms,
attentive only
to the pain of the fishhook.

Winged Fish

The fisherman raises
an underwater kite
which, stretching the line,
is lost from view
in the clouded sky.

Its resistance roots
the trees in the clouds,
turning the mountains
in the distance upside down
like a wolf's tits.

When the line breaks
the world has made one complete turn.
And the overturned dock
rests in its place,
a table with legs sticking up.

The fisherman reels in the line.
The fish, unrestrained,
tastes the painful
triumph which freedom
leaves in its mouth.

Screams

After a lifetime
of stifling the scream
against inflated pillows,
an oversight, and the pain
escapes shrieking
like air from a balloon,
availing itself of the doleful
axles of a cart.

The Night Watchman

Gently with one finger
you go around the house
and close the eyelids
of the dead rooms
until the electrical darkness
is complete.

Among the mausoleums of the furniture
burn the wayward will o'the wisps
of the cat.

The night watchman blinks
and hears himself say:
Yesterday will happen
what happened tomorrow.

Night

Dusk comes like dawn
in reverse,
receding into the night.

And when the night falls
no one knows
whether he opens or closes his eyes,
whether he dresses or undresses,
whether he gets up or lies down.

No one knows whether he comes or goes,
whether he opens or closes the door,
whether these are the dreams of yesterday
or the nightmares of tomorrow.

Dusk

Past a brick house
drive a white car,
a green, orange
and red bus,
and a tanker truck;

a bit later a black taxi
with a yellow roof;

and the lights go on
of a white car,
a green, orange
and red bus,
a tanker truck
and a black taxi
with a yellow roof,

miles away
from the brick house.

Driver

The driver of the hearse
parks in front of the church;
he feeds coins into the meter.
With a sigh or a yawn
he leafs through the newspaper.
Everything goes better on wheels.
The drive to the cemetery
is serene and sober.
The worst part are the stops,
the fuss kicked up by the relatives,
the ceremonies, the speeches.
Apart from that, it's a good job.

Travellers of the Future

The children know the names
of all the cars
on the highway.
But when I ask them
the names of the distant
but visible stars
where they dream of travelling
in spacecraft faster than light,
they shrug their shoulders.

Tunnel

Like a bullet
its barrel
an automobile
leaves the tunnel
and enters
the dazzling
temple
of life.

Blaaam!

At the bottom of the ravine:
Blaaam!
                Intertwined,
                                deaf
to the interminable horn
on which their chests lie,
two lovers' bodies.

Myths

The hen, the cow, the pig
are unlikely animals;
trademark logotypes.
Everything happens in the refrigerator
between sunset and sunrise:
the liquid of the eggs
sets in ice cube trays
with dozens of hollows.
The bacon, sliced all by itself,
falls off the thick walls.
While we dream, speaking
in dead languages,
mooing, cackling, grunting,
the refrigerator is milking the moon.
Have you perhaps not heard its hallucinated
humming in your sleep?
And when we wake up
the eggs and the bacon await us, fried,
and a glass of fresh and cold milk.

Refrigerator

Behind the shop window
it opens the door
and shows the interior
filled with food
of rubber and fruit of wax
and closes it;
it opens its door,
shows the interior
filled with food
of rubber and fruit of wax
and closes it;
and some go on,
but others
always stop
fascinated
to see how the refrigerator
opens the door
and shows the interior
filled with food
of rubber and fruit of wax
and closes it;
opens its door,
shows the interior
filled with food
of rubber and fruit of wax
and closes it . . .

Child

Centuries later,
when only the shells are left
of a society
that consumed itself,
they will find the remains
of a little Pharoah
in a broken refrigerator
buried
under pyramids of debris.

Menu

You should be like the turkey,
gobbling up filthy spiders,
lethal paints for granaries
or blond diamond fragments,
to get accustomed
to the tender meat of the animal
fattened on flowers
from radioactive feed.

Caution. Tomorrow or the day after
they will appear on the menu
as the only dish of the day.

Antiquarian

The collector of iridescences
walks through the street picking up
the crushed jellyfish of oil,
scraping the shells of mollusks,
trapping in his butterfly net
the bubble of soap
with its familiar window;

plucking the sunbathed neck
of the defunct pigeon
and the plumage of the hummingbird,
embalmed and suspended
in its turbulent flight
as in a diorama. (Its eggs,
hollow, were the size
of a white coffee bean).

Spectral banalities, visual
garbage; rubble from
the bridge of the rainbow
which has fallen into disuse,
coming down everywhere in pieces.

Monument

This bombed-out gas station
which Pop Art reproduced
at the time almost photographically
and of which the poets sang
in objective verses,
resisted heroically, like those legendary
Western forts, during the siege
by the hordes of highway pirates.

The tanker truck
with its escort and reinforcements
never arrived at its destination;
it was intercepted on the road
which is now tangled with roots,
and fell with its freight
of black gold into the hands
of motorcycle gangs.

This monolith
shaped like an oil tower and this plaque
commemorate those days of the breakdown,
a landmark among the ruins, surrounded
by charred cars.

Fuel

A fingerprint
in the form of a nebula
belonging to an immense thumb
pointing down
rubs with its tip the skyscrapers
of blacked-out capitals,
uselessly turning
the toothed wheel
of a lighter without fuel.
The ground stone has
the shape and size of the earth.
And its sparks seem like stars.

Grey Areas

Someone ventures
into grey areas, deserted
but intensely illuminated,
where in endless tunnels,
under eyeless lights,
echoes multiply
a scream of horror.

Poker

Everything was abandoned
hurriedly
like the cards
and bets
of a poker game
at the fire department.

So far no one has returned,
and the fire was put out
long ago.

Highway

On the highway, empty
as the artery of a corpse,
something pink
rolling in the wind;

a doll's leg.

Airport

Fantasmal seagulls
glide over the scars
of the plain: grey runways
at the abandoned airport
where the purple beacons
still blink at dusk,
absurd highways signs
leading to the cliffs.

A young tree has made a way for itself
and grows by cracking the concrete.
It is bent over from the wind
that comes impetuously from the sea.

The Jewellery Store

A strident burglar alarm
rings at the jewellery store.
The wind tears up
the special edition of a newspaper
over which hands were fighting
a few years or days ago.

The alarm bell was set off
perhaps by the heavy breathing
of a dying rat.
No one has come to turn it off.
It rings and rings in an empty street.

In the semi-darkness of the sealed
vaults, the diamonds sparkle
on black velvet,
uselessly safe.
They are worth no more
than the shattered panes
of the shopwindows
that litter the sidewalks.

The earth is an enormous raw diamond
laboriously ground by the stars.

IV.

Virus

The word is a virus.

William S. Burroughs

Epidemic

You need
several million viruses
to obtain a visible dot.
And several million dots
to obtain a single line.
How many million lines!
How many million dots!
How many million viruses!

Reserve

I am deaf
to the garrulousness of the agraphics.
I am blind
to the literariness of the graphomaniacs.
Fewer and fewer words
are incrusted into paper by my pen.

Fewer and fewer words
come from my mouth, muzzled
by the moustache that sews up my lips
with hundreds of greying stitches.

Virus*

If you carry the poison
in your jaws,
bite your tail
where the antidote is,
like the ouroboros.

* "Viper's humour" in Greek

Vaccination

In reality I am no longer writing,
I am inoculating vowels, consonants
of an alphabet of microbes.
With the virus of verbiage
I inoculate the silence.

Clean Slate

The virus of smallness
which once was a vaccine,
an antigen for hodgepodge,
has now become a plague.
Fight it with formalin
or ultraviolet light.
Preface it with a mute h.
Silence this son of a bitch.

Dead Letter

A virus in action
is almost invisible,
the light streamlines its body.
It can readily be observed
under an electron
microscope only
after it is dead.

Stuffed Mosquito

You are stuffing maximum meaning
into a tiny place: ambrosia
into a mosquito's guts,
in order to dot
the i's, put a full stop
to the word *life*, to the word
end, with its exalting excrement.

Nursing Assistant

You practice with the ball-point pen
and its retractible tip
like the nursing assistant
with the hypodermic needle:
injecting air bubbles
and extracting juice
from the porous word *orange*.

Fountain Pen

Working the air
bubbles you make
with spittle
and a fountain pen
you have so far achieved
sponges and at most
foam on blotting paper.

Acorn Juice

You whip drool. You foam
exudations overwhelmed
by the excessive use of words.
And with the glossy
juice of the gland
you transcribe some revived
repeated words.

Lead Sheets

You turn the pages,
grey and heavy
as lead,
from being all white
so long, waiting
in the golden dusk.

Short Shrift

They appear to move mountains
and shrink seas,
to deviate rivers. To found cities
in the moonlight,
when they write gigantic
insignificances
on the wallpaper,
between four walls,
these enormous shadow fingers.

Ivory Rabbits

In scarce white
space mate
concentrated verses,
without *horror vacui*,
growing hard
like teeth
mounting one another.

Parking Taxis

These letter vehicles
start moving
when read successively
like parked taxis
pushed on by their drivers.

Without starting the engine,
to save gas,
they occupy the spot left free
by those who have driven away.

And after the trip
these letter vehicles
return and wait right here
for the same or other readers.

Readers

You moisten your fingertip.
You turn the page
and the soot of burned eyelashes
from a typographic butterfly
with smeared scaly wings
remains on the skin of your fingers.

You turn the pages with your eyes closed
and imprint the spiral ridges
of the fingerprint seal, the ocelli,
into the pulsating fluttering paper.

The dusk is the dawn
of the creatures of the night
and our midnight their midday.
Their vision becomes keener
as our blindness increases.

And in the darkness our hands
are open like books;
they turn our palms like pages
and their eyes follow a few lines
without much interest in their fate.

Self-Portraits

Your poems suffered
the effects of Thalidomide.
Born with verses missing
and mutilated strophes,
they are now adults and describe
their handicaps with their feet;
with confident brushstrokes
guided by the incisors,
with tongue and lips
they paint their self-portraits.

Condemned Highrise

This text smells of moldy elevator,
a few echoes huddling in a corner.

Rumination

Like chewing gum that has lost
its taste and aroma long ago
you once more revise
this bland, amorphous and colourless
text which at this point
only tastes and smells
of the tongue that is kneading it,
of the teeth chewing it.

Lament

You barely manage to write
on the back of a torn off
calendar leaf
about the time
you don't have to write
in a hurry, standing up, a lament.

Paleography

You return to some pronouncements
written haphazardly
who knows when, apparently
by your own hand.
You put them under the magnifying glass
before typing them with electric
pinpricks for the insect collection.
Hybrids of a febrile forehead
and a shaky wrist:
ticks pried loose
with tweezers from the skin
of a domesticated bovine language.

Expired Aspiration

To get to write some day
with the simplicity
of the cat
who cleans his fur
with a bit of saliva.

Shipwrecked

Minuscule shipwreck survivor,
your solitude is immense.
Your ocean
is a drop of water,
your island a freckle with palm trees.

Superstition

Floods and earthquakes
force you to move
from house to house.
Tyrannies from country to country.
You never get your hair cut
twice at the same barbershop.

It's a superstition.

You return to visit some
peaceful tree-lined streets
where every year the mulberry trees
retint their shadows
with the juice of ripe fruit,
just to redeem
a few lines you had forgotten
to jot down and which revive
instantly as if they had been waiting
to be rescued.

Postcard

There is nothing like the sun
for the ear. Its voice
perhaps or its silence,
but both are missing.

The round and clear
letters of its postcard
are the first luminaries
which the solitary sleeper,
blinded by his dreams, sees
again when regaining his sight.

Mother Tongue

You recall a few loose words
from the jargon of death.
They belong to your mother tongue
which you have forgotten, like a child
raised in exile.

Nickname

The O is playable.
Robert Indiana

When you find
your name insignificant,
your minimal pseudonym is
the O of *No*, the O of *Owl*,
the O of *World*.

Detritus

Among the debris
that the creek sweeps on
towards the end of winter
one finds the remains
of a decaying alphabet.

As proof this button:
an O with two dots in it
and a filament of black thread.
A bit further down, the bleached
E of a belt buckle
that used to hold a raincoat.

Microscopic Enigma

In the drop of water
that springs tremblingly
from the edge of the tap
you discern an old man
coming closer
with great difficulty,
leaning on a bacterium.
And in the next drop
that falls, the Sphinx.

Absence

Writing is originally the language of absence.
Sigmund Freud

The scale has returned to zero
and the plants on it
have vanished without a trace.

The smell of toast floats in the air.
The kitchen is getting cold.
The wicker chairs are creaking still.

The water is dripping,
but would like to run,
as when the tap was open.

The soap desires cold water
and the skin of a pair of hands
getting dirty right now.

The towel, hung up, waits
to dry another face sometime
whose image the mirror remembers.

Its cloth is green and glossy
like the lawn outside under the sun.
The comb retains some hairs.

The recently abandoned house
has the morning and the afternoon,
the whole day, still ahead of it.

The unmade bed awaits,
with the book, the arrival
of the night and its sleeper.

Time flows
smoothly and silently
in the absence, like oil.

The Invalid Writes with Green Ink

The steam of his invisible voice
fogs up the window pane
just like my invalid eyes
glued to his loquatious back.
They are watering the garden.
The ardour of language
does not touch the landscape
which it defines so well.
And when it retreats, the voice
is the moisture of green ink.

Combatant

Wanting
to fight
with the pen
you write
dynamite
moistened
with ink.

Bats

It is impossible to count the
number of bats in an ink stain.

Gregory Bateson

I.

You push away the sheets
of paper, it is useless
to get up today,
the words, blind
and sure like bats,
are sleeping in your cavernous
throat, heads down.

II.

Night falls and though mute
you see the bat of the lake
toasting the flight
with the drop of blood
stolen from you by a mosquito.

The Hare

In the iris of Dürer's
alert hare
resting in the grass
there is a painted window,
and in her window, so tiny
as to be almost invisible,
an imaginary woman
with humid eyes.

Compassion

You unscrew the wide angle
to screw on the zoom lens
as if the black camera were
a great nut and the lenses
screws of different sizes.
You measure the evening light, focus
and photograph a bent-over man,
sobbing in a square.

Studio Visit

All your titles are names
of pictures. There is much
treason discreetly
arranged against the walls.

Other challenges are still
on the easels awaiting completion.
I believe in your blank canvasses.

The Old Pony

Why are you so short?
F. Hölderlin, *Die Kürze*

The short poem has been
our battle horse. The old
pony has been worked almost to death
by the use and abuse
of its obese and obsessed riders.

It has been ridden
by epigrammatic horsemen
of all breeds;
Ezra revolving ad nauseum
in the secular Chinese carrousel;
Bertold the didascalic Bavarian
leaving for exile
mounted in its saddle.

Half the world
rode it and made it gallop
without respite, food or drink.

Dismount before it dies on you:
let it graze freely and expire in peace
in a suburban soccer field,
blowing dust balls
near gypsy tents.

And when the hapless nag dies
let's dissect it, stuff it with sawdust
for equestrian children and old poets
to have their photographs taken in the squares,
looking at the camera over its shoulder
with sad and green glass eyes.

Blue Line Taxi

There is a black Blue Line taxi
waiting for me
like a dot on the map
at Ottawa airport,
parked across from the glass tunnel
that awaits my steps
in order to open, automatically.

Its driver had been reading the paper
and is now watching how the photoelectric
door shudders,
but does not open.
It must be the wind, he thinks
in Arabian English. He
looks at his watch. No plane
arrives at this hour,
and he continues to read.

Boneless

Encouraged only
by the warm fog
of his own breath,
and his burning eyes
his only visible part,
the verbal Husky
digs and digs
in the page of snow,
but never buries his bone.

The Flour Mill's Seal

The miller's sheets are
made of flour sacks, and his pillow
cases and his curtains
and tablecloths, the woman's underskirts
and the children's underwear.
Of white and warm cotton the diapers,
the towels, the napkins and handkerchiefs.
And on everything the flour mill's seal.

Entropy

We the crazy cancer cells
extirpated from the body
which we left in the hands of quacks
who managed to make it
more cancer-ridden than ever
have returned to take charge of the chaos.

Geotropism

Like roots
on the smoked panes
of an underground window
you trace the tracks of your growth.

Going deeper towards the centre
under the foundation and a downpour
of leaden seeds, you drill
among the stones and the dead.

Fruitless

We have been presaging each other
like a pair of orphaned twins
adopted by different parents.
Like two worms we have opened
tunnels through the same apple.
Our reciprocal search
has so far been fruitless.

Paper

Motel of the pen,
hospital of the ink
birth and death certificate:
diaper and shroud.

The Word

To love it and unlove it:
discovery and loss.
To arm it and disarm it:
apprenticeship and ennui.

Index of Titles

Index of Titles

Index of Titles

Index of Titles

Index of Titles